Practical Guide to SAP® GTS
Part I

Kevin Riddell
Rajen Iyer

Thank you for purchasing this book from Espresso Tutorials!

Like a cup of espresso coffee, Espresso Tutorials SAP books are concise and effective. We know that your time is valuable and we deliver information in a succinct and straightforward manner. It only takes our readers a short amount of time to consume SAP concepts. Our books are well recognized in the industry for leveraging tutorial-style instruction and videos to show you step by step how to successfully work with SAP.

Check out our YouTube channel to watch our videos at
https://www.youtube.com/user/EspressoTutorials.

If you are interested in SAP Finance and Controlling, join us at
http://www.fico-forum.com/forum2/
to get your SAP questions answered and contribute to discussions.

Related titles from Espresso Tutorials:

▶ Claudia Jost: First Steps in the SAP® Purchasing Processes (MM)
http://5016.espresso-tutorials.com

▶ Matthew Johnson: SAP® Material Master—A Practical Guide
http://5028.espresso-tutorials.com

▶ Björn Weber: First Steps in the SAP® Production Processes (PP)
http://5027.espresso-tutorials.com

▶ Tobias Götz, Anette Götz: Practical Guide to Transportation Management with SAP®
http://5082.espresso-tutorials.com

▶ Avijt Dutta & Shreekant Shiralkar: Demand Planning with SAP® APO—Concepts and Design
http://5105.espresso-tutorials.com

▶ Avijt Dutta & Shreekant Shiralkar: Demand Planning with SAP® APO—Execution
http://5106.espresso-tutorials.com

Kevin Riddell & Rajen Iyer
Practical Guide to SAP® GTS, Part I

ISBN:	978-1-50861344-2
Editor:	Alice Adams
Proofreading:	Christine Parizo
Cover Design:	Philip Esch, Martin Munzel
Cover Photo:	fotolia: #59440955 © dashadima
Interior Design:	Johann-Christian Hanke

All rights reserved.

1st Edition 2015, Gleichen

© 2015 by Espresso Tutorials GmbH

URL: *www.espresso-tutorials.com*

Feedback
We greatly appreciate any kind of feedback you have concerning this book. Please mail us at *info@espresso-tutorials.com*.

Table of Contents

Preface

Thank you for purchasing Book 1 of the Practical Guide to SAP GTS. Our practical guide is the first of its kind for GTS. Similar guides have been written for other SAP modules, but we feel this addresses a very real business need for GTS users. If you are a current user, you already know what a powerful a tool GTS is. This book will help you use that tool more efficiently, and maybe even learn some new aspects of the system you were not familiar with.

GTS is a compliance tool. For this reason, our practical guide offers not only software assistance, but also compliance assistance. We trust that the material will assist you as you develop and/or review your own company's compliance programs. We also offer suggestions on how to audit the effectiveness of your GTS installation—ensuring you can withstand any external audit should it ever occur.

Book 1 focusses on compliance management, with an in depth review of sanctioned party list (SPL) screening. Book 2 covers customs management and preference processing. It is our hope that the multi- book format will allow you to choose the topics that you need the most.

In addition to its core content, this book offers a glimpse at GTS 11.0. Book 2 includes a review of the new Fiori Apps and UX (user experience) developments.

Thank you again and we sincerely hope this book helps make your life easier, and more compliant!

We have added a few icons to highlight important information. These include:

Tips

Tips highlight information concerning more details about the subject being described and/or additional back-ground information.

Examples

Examples help illustrate a topic better by relating it to real world scenarios.

Attention

Attention notices draw attention to information that you should be aware of when you go through the examples from this book on your own.

Finally, a note concerning the copyright: All screenshots printed in this book are the copyright of SAP SE. All rights are reserved by SAP SE. Copyright pertains to all SAP images in this publication. For simplification, we will not mention this specifically underneath every screenshot.

Introduction

Well, if that's you, this guide is here to help. Not just for SPL (Sanctioned Party Lists), but also for other key functions in SAP GTS. This book is the first of a two-part set. Part 1 focuses on compliance management and is divided into two parts—SPL and import/export compliance management. Part 2 focuses on customs management and preference processing.

There are several books on installing and configuring SAP GTS, but until now, none of those have focused on using GTS in a compliant manner. Installation and configuration are essential parts of a GTS implementation, but they are not the complete story. They also should not be the first tasks that occur in an implementation. They must be preceded by an understanding of the problems that GTS presents a solution for. You will only be able to maximize the value of a SAP GTS implementation by first conducting a thorough review of your business needs and a proper understanding of what GTS can do.

This book is meant to be a hybrid: while it is, of course, an SAP GTS manual, it is also serves as a compliance guide. SAP GTS is a software tool. The greater goal is not merely a software installation but the implementation of a complete trade compliance solution. This cannot be done solely in the area of a software implementation; it must accompany and be guided by compliance expertise. This book will help you both with a successful GTS implementation and with compliance.

This book will cover the following topics specific to SPL and compliance management:

- ▶ Understanding the regulatory requirements related to international trade compliance. These notes are focused primarily on the US but also touch on the requirements for other countries.
- ▶ Understanding how GTS can provide a solution to regulatory requirements.
- ▶ Reviews and walk-through of configuration, especially in situations where configuration choices could affect compliance levels.
- ▶ Tips on how to best leverage SAP GTS, including an overview of the key functions and the most commonly encountered user choices/actions. This is not meant to be an exhaustive review of all functions, just those that the majority of users can expect to encounter.
- ▶ Compliance tips, including specific software tips and general compliance tips.
- ▶ Suggested business process flows to assist the reader in creating similar processes at their own company.

We will not cover all of the SAP GTS functionality available. Rather than give high-level coverage of all areas, we will instead offer in-depth assistance with the specific functions a majority of users face. Each installation is free to activate the functions they wish to use and leave others unused. Based on the majority of installations, the following four general functions are covered:

- ▶ Sanctioned party list screening (Book 1)
- ▶ Compliance management (Book 1)

▶ Preference processing (Book 2)

▶ Customs management (Book 2)

Each book also includes a section on SAP GTS Version 11.0 and the changes and improvements that it brings, as well as appendixes with useful references for the reader.

Throughout the book, there are references to *SAP ERP* (Enterprise Resource Planning) and *SAP ECC* (SAP ERP Central Component). SAP GTS work best when it is integrated with an ERP program. For the purposes of simplicity, we assume that it is always SAP in this book. It should be noted, however, that SAP GTS can be integrated with non-SAP ERP programs as well.

This book is useful for a wide range of companies at various stages of creating a compliance solution, including:

▶ Companies unfamiliar with international trade compliance requirements who want to increase their knowledge of regulatory guidelines.

▶ Companies evaluating the most appropriate trade compliance solution for them.

▶ Companies committed to GTS who want to understand its functionality better before installation begins.

▶ Companies currently implementing GTS seeking to base their configuration decisions on a solid understanding of their purpose and implications.

▶ Companies using GTS who are considering activating software features not previously used or who want assistance in developing an internal training program.

As you can see, this book is intended for multiple audiences at various stages of an implementation project. It is our hope that this book will assist you in your project and lead to a higher level of compliance! However, it must be noted that this book does not offer legal advice. The regulatory compliance discussions are meant to raise awareness; specific answers to your company's questions on regulatory compliance must be directed to your company's legal advisor or expert counsel.

We hope you will find this book as informative and educational as we have found writing it!

1 Sanctioned party list screening

One of the most commonly used functions in SAP GTS is *sanctioned party list screening*, or *SPL checking*. SPL checking means that all of your business partners and documents will be checked against known lists of sanctioned or restricted parties. What exactly is a sanctioned/restricted party, and what does it mean for your business?

1.1 Introduction

Everyone understands what a country embargo is; in other words, you may not deal with that country. For example, US companies cannot do business with North Korean companies. However, it is not as well known that government agencies more often embargo individuals and entities than they do countries. For example, the US Department of the Treasury lists entities in certain countries, such as Libya, that it considers a danger to the national interests of the United States. As a result, a US company may not sell to any of the listed companies or individuals. The lists of forbidden or restricted parties are called *Sanctioned Party Lists*, or *SPL*.

SPL lists are commonly thought of an "export" issue, and most companies understand they must ensure they never export to a listed entity. However, these lists can apply to imports as well as domestic activity. Buying from or selling to a person in your own country could violate certain SPL rules; for example, there are US entities on many of the lists.

It is critical that your business protects itself from liability and screens all of its business partners against the published lists. A system must be set up that checks *business partners (BP)* as soon as they are created or edited and checks the partners within documents. Any time the system thinks that it has found a match, it will block the partner or document from use until an authorized user reviews it. That user will make a decision on the block, i.e., is it really a match, or just a close call? If it is just a close call, they can release the partner/document. If it is a real match, it will remain blocked.

In the next section, we will review the suggested settings, best practices, and user tips for SAP GTS SPL functionality. It is not intended to be exhaustive but rather covers the most commonly used areas of the software, as well as those most likely to cause confusion.

Before we begin, we would like to explain the way SAP GTS SPL works on a high level. To illustrate, we will look at three simple process flows, including:

▶ How an SPL match is determined.

▶ How a business partner block is determined and managed.

▶ How a document block is determined and managed.

Figure 1.1, Figure 1.2, and Figure 1.3 display these processes in the form of a flow chart. These simple flows are not meant to capture all SAP GTS functionality but rather to provide a high-level overview of its three core competencies: determining a match, blocking a partner that matches, and blocking a document containing a matched partner. For example, there are many more settings available to fine-tune the match logic than what is shown. By reviewing this diagram, you will better be able to understand where the other features fit in and how they affect the outcome of checks.

Let's look at a couple of key terms. When a user reviews a match, they must decide if they are looking at a *true positive* or a *false positive*. A true positive is an actual match, and the business partner is the SPL entity. A false positive means the system found that the two were close enough to warrant a block, but upon review, it has been determined that the match is not real.

This chapter dives into each of these areas in more depth, as well as covers areas not shown in these diagrams. Lastly, it wraps up with a general discussion on SPL compliance and tips for meeting the expected compliance standard.

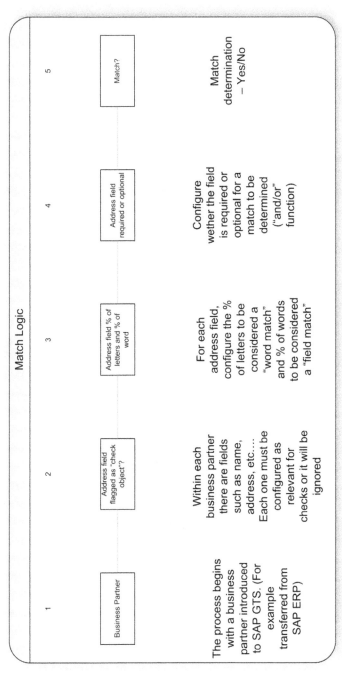

Figure 1.1: Match logic

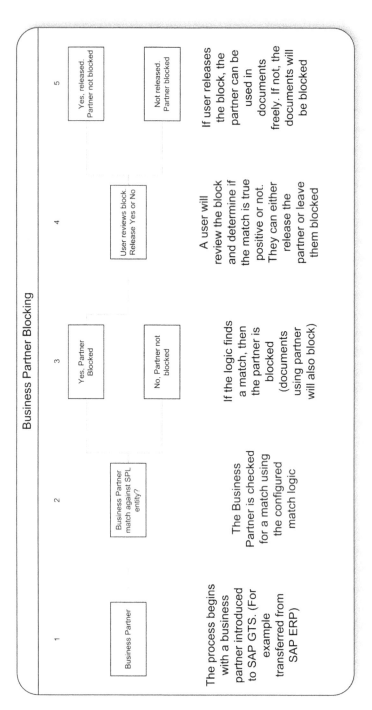

Figure 1.2: Business partner blocking

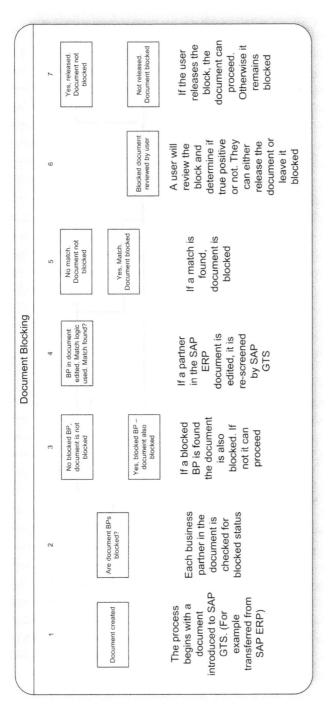

Figure 1.3: Document blocking

1.2   Configuration

SPL screening involves screening your business partner (BP) against lists of SPL uploaded to SAP GTS as XML files. Third party companies provide this content as a service and send you updates when the government updates the list. SPL involves screening text or characters, which is very performance intensive. To address this, SAP GTS allows you to build an index of denied party list (SPL) content. Business partners use this index to improve screening performance.

The indexing function is addressed in SAP GTS master data (see Section 1.7.3). Indexing is important. As the system runs sanctioned party list screening, it breaks down the SPL master data and business partner data into search terms and only compares the generated search terms during screening. This reduces the runtime of sanctioned party list screening significantly.

SAP GTS provides you with many options and flexibility for SPL Screening. It can adjust to match the business needs of any organization based on its risk exposure and business activity. This sort of flexibility is available through multiple settings from which each installation can choose. There are two key areas of configuration that determine these settings: (a) control settings, which influence the way SPL functionality functions, and (b) control procedures, which allow you to set certain rules within user control, such as exclusion, alias, etc.

All of the content and screens shown in Section 1.2 are configuration and accessed through the following menu path: SPRO • SAP REFERENCE IMG • GLOBAL TRADE SERVICES • COMPLIANCE MANAGEMENT • SANCTIONED PARTY LIST SCREENING.

1.2.1   Control settings (Part 1)

To maximize the comparison index effectiveness, it is important that you ensure that the SPL controls for the index are set correctly. Use transaction SPRO or follow menu path SAP REFERENCE IMG • SAP GLOBAL TRADE SERVICES • SAP COMPLIANCE MANAGEMENT • SANCTIONED PARTY LIST SCREENING SERVICE • CONTROL SETTINGS FOR SANCTIONED PARTY LIST SCREENING.

Once in the CONTROL SETTINGS area, highlight the SPL Legal Regulation (i.e., SPLUS) and click on DETAILS 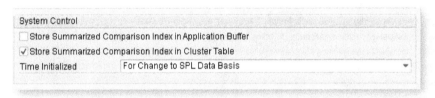. Let's review the key sections in this area.

System control

Make sure that STORE SUMMARIZED COMPARISON INDEX IN APPLICATION BUFFER and STORE SUMMARIZED COMPARISON INDEX IN CLUSTER TABLE are selected (see Figure 1.4). These system controls improve the search response because, if the system first uses the application buffer and does not find the entry, it searches in the cluster table. Note that checking the application buffer check box calls for more system memory resources. If you have fewer system resources and are not that particular about the search response, then you can uncheck the application buffer option and only use the cluster table option to store the index.

TIME INITIALIZED: Select FOR CHANGE TO SPL DATA BASIS from the dropdown menu to ensure that any update to DPL content triggers SPL screening.

System Control	
☐ Store Summarized Comparison Index in Application Buffer	
☑ Store Summarized Comparison Index in Cluster Table	
Time Initialized	For Change to SPL Data Basis ▾

Figure 1.4: System control settings

Scope of check

In the CONSIDER VALIDITY field, select the third option from the drop down menu INCLUDE BOTH VALID FROM AND VALID TO DATE (see Figure 1.5). This validity check keeps track of SPL entries that drop off the SPL list. This selection notes whether you want to see matches against expired SPL entities (i.e., do you want to know if your customer used to be on an SPL list?).

If you have a business partner with multiple addresses, select the MULTIPLE ADDRESS CHECK ACTIVE check box.

If you want expired records to be marked for deletion, you can check the SET DELETION INDICATOR ACCORDING TO OFFICIAL VALIDITY check box.

CHECK LOGIC FOR DOCS: Maintain the default setting NEW CHECK OF CHANGED ADDRESSES. This ensures that the document partner addresses are screened when they are changed in the document. If the addresses are not changed, the system refers to the business partner master screen results.

SEARCH STRATEGY: Select the first option from the dropdown menu SPL ENTRY SEARCHES IN ADDRESS AND VICE VERSA. This setting ensures that SPL screening is performed by both selecting the entry in the SPL and finding a match in the business partner list, and also by taking a business partner address and performing the screening against the SPL.

SIZE OF CHECK PACKAGE: Maintain this size based on performance testing and sizing. For volume transfer, we normally recommend keeping the size between 5000 and 10000 for performance reasons. Of course, you must decide if this works for your total number of partners.

Figure 1.5: SPL scope of check set up

Three pitfalls to be aware of in control settings

 Be very careful about selecting the Cross-Check Active box in Figure 1.5—this functionality might result in more hits because it cross-checks the name against other elements such as street and city characters. It will search for field contents in all other fields. For example, if the SPL entity was "Kevin Riddell on GTS Street," this may hit against a BP of "Kevin GTS on Riddell Street." This should only be used if your master data is not clean and fields such as name, street, etc. are not consistently used. If you have disciplined data, this is best left unchecked.

Also, avoid checking the Include Master Records Flagged for Deletion box unless absolutely necessary. A better option is to use the archive functionality.

We recommend that you select the Take Past Check Results into Account box. This will help the system remember your decisions on the false positives and prevent reviewing the same results multiple times.

Audit

In order to save time, we recommend that you uncheck all Write Audit boxes during the initial conversion (i.e., when the production system is set up, but prior to go-live when you transfer the data), if you have a large volume of business partner records. Writing to the audit trail file takes additional processing time, and the business partner conversion might run for hours. Once the business partner records are transferred, you can check the boxes to capture the audit trails.

Notification

SPL configuration allows you to send a notification if documents are blocked due to SPL screening. Check the SEND MAIL WHEN DOCUMENT BLOCKED option if you want to send an email when the document is blocked (see Figure 1.6). Check the SEND MAIL WHEN BUSINESS PARTNER BLOCKED option if you want to send a notification when the business partner is blocked.

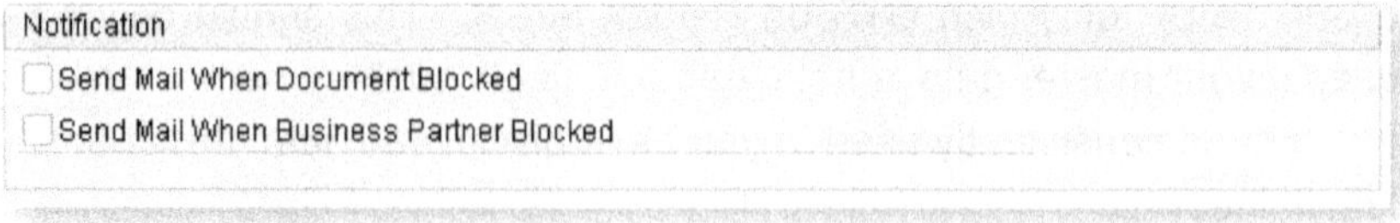

Notification
☐ Send Mail When Document Blocked
☐ Send Mail When Business Partner Blocked

Figure 1.6: Notification settings

Note that there is still work to be done in BASIS before this functionality will work. Set up the prerequisite steps that are part of the SAP GTS front-end cockpit setup. Use transaction /SAPSLL/MENU_LEGAL, click SYSTEM COMMUNICATION/WORKFLOW under the SYSTEM ADMINISTRATION section, and select WORKFLOW. Then, follow these steps:

1. Maintain user groups. These help you group the users to whom you would like to send the notification.

2. Under NOTIFICATION CONTROL FOR BLOCKED DOCUMENTS, maintain the foreign trade organization, legal regulation (e.g., SPLUS), and user groups you maintained in the previous step.

We will return to CONTROL SETTINGS shortly, but first it makes sense to discuss the CONTROL PROCEDURE

1.2.2   Control procedure

Another important control within the configuration is the control procedure to compare addresses. This configuration is in menu path SAP REFERENCE IMG • SAP GLOBAL TRADE SERVICES • SAP COMPLIANCE MANAGEMENT • SANCTIONED PARTY LIST SCREENING SERVICE • DEFINE CONTROL PROCEDURE FOR ADDRESS COMPARISON.

There are three sections to set up in this control procedure: Control Structure, Detail Control, and Assign Address Fields.

Control structure

See Figure 1.7 for an overview of the control structure. Select the appropriate LANGUAGE FOR COMPARISON (e.g., English).

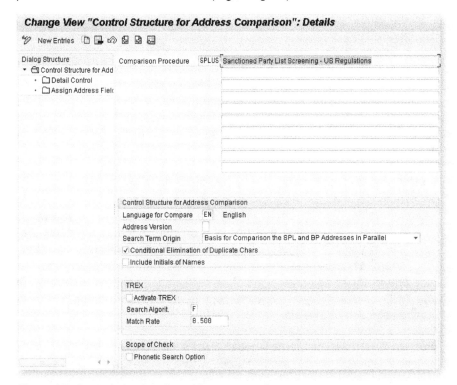

Figure 1.7: Control structure for address comparison

In the field SEARCH TERM ORIGIN, there are three choices:

1. BASIS FOR COMPARISON EXCLUSIVELY FROM SANCTIONED PARTY LIST. This ensures that your screening is performed against the SPL content. This means that the system will take the SPL words and look for them in the BP address.

2. BASIS FOR COMPARISON EXCLUSIVELY FROM BUSINESS PARTNER: In this model, the system will take the BP words and look for them in the SPL entry.

3. BASIS FOR COMPARISON THE SPL AND BP ADDRESS IN PARALLEL: In this scenario, the system will look in both directions (BP in SPL and SPL in BP), and both results must meet the required thresholds. This generally will reduce your hit count.

If you want to activate TREX, select the Activate box under TREX.

TREX is an optional functionality that allows for more robust searching tools in SAP GTS (see Section 1.4 to learn more).

Detail control

In this control, you first list the name and address fields that you want to consider for screening and the logic (AND or OR). With AND logic, the field is considered for screening against the same fields, and results are used for comparison. With OR logic, there needs to be more than one field, so it takes the result from all the OR fields for the final success or hit (see Figure 1.9).

Define the business partner address fields that are relevant for SPL screening, as well as the logical operator you want to assign to these selected fields: AND or OR. You use the OR operation when you would like to search for a match that has one or more address elements. For example, if you have street, city, and country listed with OR operators, SPL searches return results for any business partner address that has any one of these fields as a match. On the other hand, you should use the AND operator if you want to capture individual address fields for match selection and result.

For obvious reasons, name should always be screened for your basic settings. (There may be rare instances where a non-name based screening is needed, but generally, it is important.) Country should also always be included and be an "AND" function along with name. This is because country is unique in that a blank country field will always be considered a hit. This way, you get accurate results without fear of missing a SPL listing that is not country-specific.

All of the other fields must be chosen according to your business needs and a decision made as to "OR" vs. "AND." Unlike country, requiring these fields could result in a miss if the field is blank.

Secondly, within each field, there are more detailed settings to configure. To do this, highlight one of the fields and click on the Details button 🔍.

Before we go through the steps required in the Details area, let's go through some key terms (see Figure 1.9).

The *search term* is the first step in determining a match as the system searches individual characters. If it finds a match, it then uses the *originating feature*, which is the complete word to find a match or the number of complete words in a string that are a match.

How the search term and originating features are explained

 The BP in our scenario is Rajen Iyer. The SPL is Rajen Yer Smith. The search term settings decide what percent of a word is required for the word to be considered a match. The originating feature settings decide how many words in a string must have met the search term requirement. Let us assume we have 75 percent for both search term and originating feature. In this case, we have three words, which match up as:

Rajen vs. Rajen = 100%

Iyer vs. yer = 75%

Smith vs. either Rajen or Yer = negligible – less than 75%

Therefore, we have two out of three words that meet the search term requirements of 75 percent.

Next is the originating feature check. We have two out of three words, which is 66 percent. This fails to meet the 75 percent standard, and we do not have a match.

Let us further explain the SPL screening and the mechanism behind the function. The SAP GTS SPL screening can be summarized in two steps.

Step 1: The system tries to determine a match between the individual characters with the name and address as search terms of business partner and SPL characters. All the characters have to be a match to produce a hit. Let's use the example of the name OSAMA as the business partner name and an SPL entry with same name. The system uses the business partner search term OSAMA and SPL search term OSAMA. In this case, it is a 100 percent match.

Step 2: Match the original form. Consider the original form as a complete word. For example, for the name Rajen Iyer, the search terms are the individual characters, R-A-J-E-N, and with original form, they are the complete words, Rajen and Iyer. If you get a match in Step 1 when the system searches with search criteria, you need to confirm it based on percentage settings maintained in the configuration for search terms. You calculate the percentage as follows:

▶ Search term percentage = Number of letters matched in original terms of the business partner and SPL / number of letters in the original business partner * 100.

▶ Originating feature percentage = Number of words matched / number of words in SPL entity * 100. It is only a SPL hit if both percentages match.

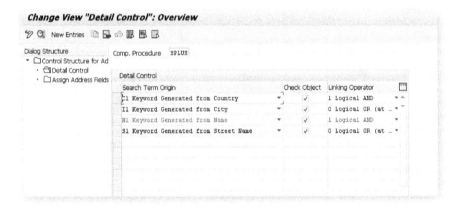

Figure 1.8: Detail control list of fields

Follow these steps for each field set up:

Step 1: The SEARCH TERM ORIGIN will default to your selection made in the CONTROL STRUCTURE earlier (see section Control structure on page 23). You can choose to override this selection by individual field or leave it unchanged.

Step 2: Ensure that CHECK OBJECT is selected. This ensures that this field will be checked.

Step 3: Make sure that the correct LINKING OPERATOR (1 Logical AND) is selected. It will be set up as you just chose in the previous section. If you prefer, you can change your choice here.

Step 4: Within the Relational Operator field, you have two choices:

- ▶ Comparison Index Contained in the Keyword from Address: With this option, the system searches for individual characters within the business partner addresses.

- ▶ Comparison Index and Keyword from Address are Identical: With this option, it considers only strings of characters. We recommend that you use this option for closer hits.

Step 5: Within Minimal Similarity, set the search term and Originating Feature percentages. Figure 1.9 shows the default selection that we recommend keeping. If you want to achieve a higher hit rate, then you can alter the percentages to see if you can achieve your goal. The option for Search Term Origin will default to the selection you chose in Control Structure, but you can change it here.

Let's look at another example. Take a case where you have a business partner named Teror A Citizen and an SPL entry for Terror T Citizen. The system first searches the individual characters within the two business partner words, Teror and Citizen. In the case of Teror, it is 5 out of 6 are a match, and the in case of Citizen, it is a complete match. Therefore, the first round of percentage threshold is the search term's qualification; with Teror, it is 83.33 percent, and with Citizen, it is 100 percent. There is no match for the middle name. Therefore, if you had the search term less than 83.33 percent, then the search term results in a successful match. Once the search term is successful, the system moves on to the Originating Feature. If the search is successful, the original terms are matched against each individual word of the business partner with the SPL entry. In this case, the Teror business partner address is matched against the Terror SPL entry and the Citizen business partner address is matched with the Citizen SPL entry. In other words, the business partner originating form name Teror A Citizen has two of three words match against the SPL entry Terror T Citizen, so the percentage for the originating terms calculates to 66.66 percent. If you have a percentage less than 66.66 percent, then only this name is found as a match.

Step 6: Select Allow Multiple Matches for Origin to consider repeated words as individual entities. Without this selection, duplicate address entries are considered as one. We recommend avoiding this option because it tends to raise the hit ratio and return more hits that are false.

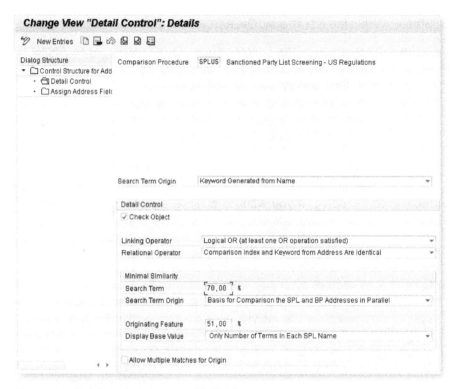

Figure 1.9: Detail control view specific field

Assign address fields

Last, click THE ASSIGN ADDRESS FIELDS folder to bring up the screen in Figure 1.10. You can see the delivered fields for SPL screening. Click the NEW ENTRIES button to add fields that you want to screen (e.g., CITY2).

This is referring to the fields from your SAP ERP Central Component (SAP ECC) system in the business partner master. There are typically multiple fields for a field category such as "Name."

You can choose to review all of the available fields for a category, such as reviewing "Name 1" through "Name 4." If you have reason to believe there is corrupt data in some of these fields, you may want to reduce the fields reviewed. For example, you could choose to look only at "Name 1" and "Name 2."

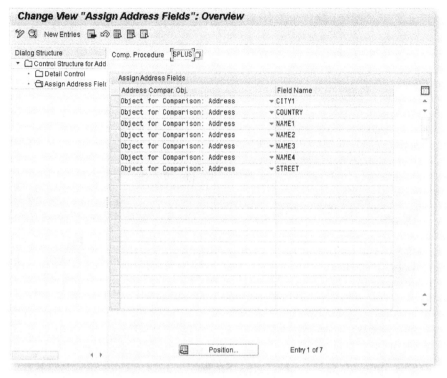

Figure 1.10: Control settings with assign address fields

Define Comparison procedure for SAP TREX

You can define the comparison in the following menu path: SAP GLOBAL TRADE SERVICES • COMPLIANCE MANAGEMENT • SANCTIONED PARTY LIST SCREENING • DEFINE COMPARISON PROCEDURE • DEFINE COMPARISON PROCEDURE FOR SAP TREX SEARCH. You can set up for CONDITIONAL ELIMINATION OF DUPLICATE CHARACTERS and can consider the abbreviations of company names that otherwise might be excluded from screening improperly.

There are two options to choose from: standard logic and extended logic. If you use standard logic, the first letter of both words being compared must be identical. This does not apply to extended logic. You can choose "F" for error-tolerant (FUZZY) screening logic and "G" for extended logic (EXTENDED FUZZY) screening logic. In the detail control use the "logical AND" operator if you want to match specific section of address (Name, City, etc.).

1.2.3 Control settings (Part 2)

Follow menu path SAP REFERENCE IMG • SAP GLOBAL TRADE SERVICES • SAP COMPLIANCE MANAGEMENT • SANCTIONED PARTY LIST SCREENING SERVICE • CONTROL SETTINGS FOR SANCTIONED PARTY LIST SCREENING to return to the control settings shown in Figure 1.11[1].

List types

The first task is to set up and review the LIST TYPES.

List types
We highly recommended that you use a subscription provider for your SPL list content. SPL lists are large and change rapidly. Attempting to maintain them manually is risky and will consume a great deal of time and effort. Subscription providers are available that will offer you this content, regularly updated, for a reasonable price. The example used in this book is MK Data Services, which offers comprehensive SPL data for GTS users. See Section 1.3 for further discussion on subscription services.

Within each list type, you can also specify a minimum and maximum length for each key address field. For example, you can have a minimum length of three for city in the "561L" list and a minimum of four for "BALK." We recommend that you stay with your subscription provider's settings if you are using a subscription service.

If you choose, you can maintain the values for name, street, and city under the MINIMUM LENGTH OF INDEX ENTRIES section. Simply click on the list in question and select the DETAILS button 🔍. If you are using a subscription service and do not want to make any changes, you can move on to reference type.

---

[1] List types shown are property of MK Data Services and used with permission

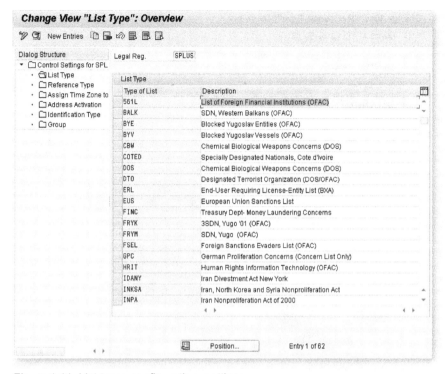

Figure 1.11: List types configuration -settings

Reference type

When you are in the control setting configuration step, click the REFER-ENCE TYPE folder to bring up the details shown in Figure 1.12. Reference types are a way to ensure accurate reading of acronyms in names. For example, if the business partner was "SAP A.K.A SAP AG" and the SPL was "SAP (Also Known As SAP AG)," you may miss this match because of the significant difference in the names. Capturing A.K.A. as shown in Figure 1.12 ensures that you will not miss this. Some data subscription providers will also provide you with suggested reference type data that can be populated automatically.

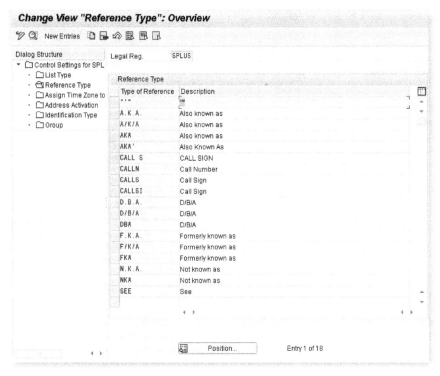

Figure 1.12: Reference types

Assign time zone

Click the ASSIGN TIME ZONE in the DEADLINE TYPE folder to bring up the screen shown in Figure 1.13. You can assign a specific time zone that will be considered when "to" and "from" dates are relevant to an SPL search.

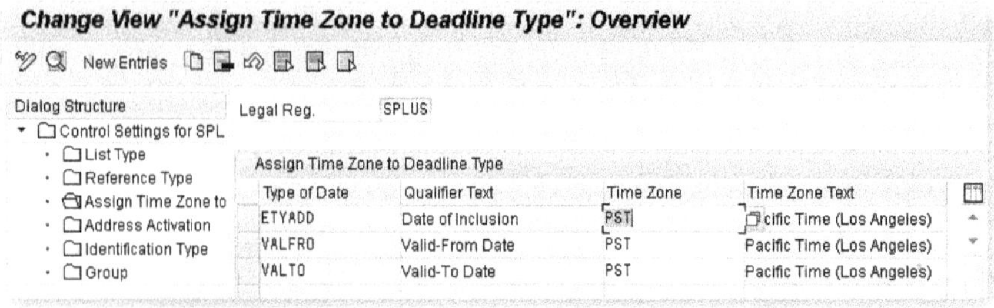

Figure 1.13: Assign time zone

Address activation

Click on the ADDRESS ACTIVATION folder to bring up the details screen shown in Figure 1.14. The system delivered address is the STANDARD ADDRESS; you can add any other address type that you prefer to the screen.

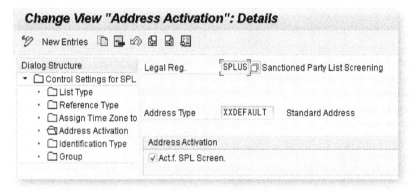

Figure 1.14: Activate address types

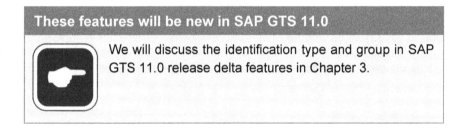

These features will be new in SAP GTS 11.0

We will discuss the identification type and group in SAP GTS 11.0 release delta features in Chapter 3.

1.2.4 Activate the business partner at the business partner function level

Follow menu path SAP REFERENCE IMG • SAP GLOBAL TRADE SERVICES • SAP COMPLIANCE MANAGEMENT • SANCTIONED PARTY LIST SCREENING SERVICE • ACTIVATE BUSINESS PARTNER AT BUSINESS PARTNER FUNCTION LEVEL (see Figure 1.15).

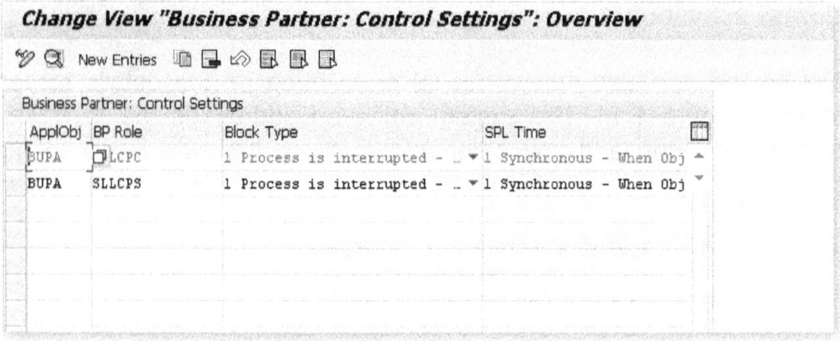

Figure 1.15: Type of SPL block

This task involves setting up the application object control settings for business partners and their associated business partner functions. The control settings involve selecting the type of SPL BLOCK (the default setting is titled 1 PROCESS IS INTERRUPTED – SYSTEM REMOVES BLOCK), the time of the SPL check (SYNCHRONOUS – WHEN OBJECT IS UPDATED), and the business area it falls under (Logistics, Financial Accounting, or Human Resources).

From here, you can highlight one of the lines and click on the DETAILS button ⬛ (see Figure 1.16).

Figure 1.16: Business partner screening control settings

The default SPL block setting means that the system screens the business partner. If it finds a block based on the system parameter settings, it blocks this business partner. Users can then review the results and manually release the block or take appropriate action. For the TIME OF SPL CHECK field, we recommend that you use SYNCHRONOUS, except during conversion or volume transfer, when you should set it to ASYNCHRONOUS. Then revert back to SYNCHRONOUS for ongoing or regular transfers.

The separation into business area (SEP. BUS. AREAS) field ensures that blocked business partners and associated transactions fall under the appropriate view for operational effectiveness and reporting. Settings are pre-delivered for customers and vendors, but you must ensure that the entries for other business partner roles (e.g., contact person, employee, or bank) are maintained. To restrict the control of review of business partners by company codes within your organization, select the check box ENHANCED AUTHORIZATION CHECK in the SANCTIONED PARTY LIST SCREENING AREA and ensure that the security profile has the FOREIGN TRADE ORGANIZATION checkbox selected.

1.2.5 Activate legal regulations

The SPL Legal Regulation must be activated to function. You can set the parameter for this activation, which can be country or a combination of country and country group (for example – you could specifically name the USA, or make a group containing the USA and Canada).

For this example, we will set up the activation by country, but the same process would apply if you choose to make country groups. Make your decision based on how many countries you are dealing with—if it is a small number, individual country makes sense. If you are dealing with dozens of countries, you may want to use groups to save time and effort (see Figure 1. for an example).

Legal regulation allows you to define the configuration within the system specific to the function (SPL, License determination, or customs declaration) within SAP GTS. To activate the SPL legal regulation by each country, you can choose from five different options:

1. Check: Dispatch (exclusively)
2. Check: Export (exclusively)
3. Check: Dispatch/Export (excluding domestic)
4. Check: Dispatch/Export (including domestic)
5. No check (no SPL service activation)

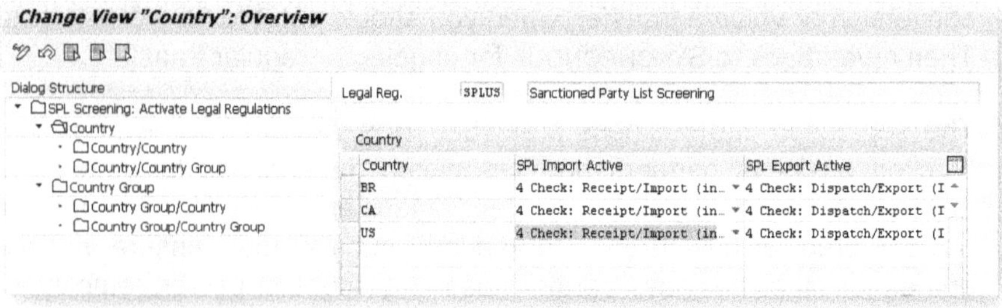

Figure 1.17: Country-level activation

We highly recommended that you choose option four, which will ensure that your domestic partners and transactions are screened, as well as your imports/exports. Many SPL lists apply domestically as well as during export. If you need to make a more narrow selection for a business reason (e.g., to reduce the number of false positive hits), be careful that what you are doing is compliant. Consider making multiple legal regulations so that you can perform domestic screening on the critical lists, and export only screening on the less sensitive ones. For a more detailed discussion of these lists, see Section 1.9.1.

1.2.6 Define reasons for releasing blocked documents and business partners

There is an optional feature in GTS that allows you to assign a *reason for release*. This feature allows the user to specify why they released a partner during their review. We recommended that you use this feature as outlined in the steps below. Adding reasons at the time of release will increase the value of the audit trail should any decisions be questioned at a later point in time.

The menu path is SAP REFERENCE IMG • SAP GLOBAL TRADE SERVICES • SAP COMPLIANCE MANAGEMENT • DEFINE REASONS FOR RELEASING BLOCKED DOCUMENTS AND BUSINESS PARTNERS.

In this screen, you can enter a NEW ENTRY, or pull up the list of current entries by choosing OPTIONS FOR RELEASE REASON. Current options can be edited and/or deleted. Figure 1.18 is an example of a list of reasons. Each business must choose its own reasons, and this is intended only as an example to give you some ideas. GTS does not come loaded with reasons, and they must be set up if you want to use them.

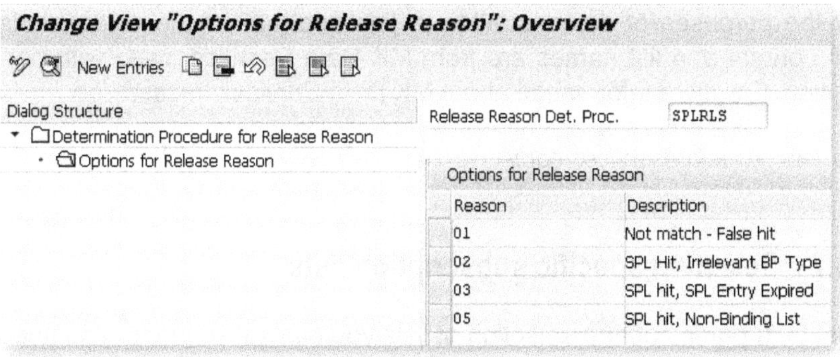

Change View "Options for Release Reason": Overview

New Entries

Dialog Structure

▼ ☐ Determination Procedure for Release Reason
  • ☐ Options for Release Reason

Release Reason Det. Proc.   SPLRLS

Options for Release Reason

Reason	Description
01	Not match - False hit
02	SPL Hit, Irrelevant BP Type
03	SPL hit, SPL Entry Expired
05	SPL hit, Non-Binding List

Figure 1.18: Release reasons

1.3   Subscription service

We highly recommended that you subscribe to a data provider for your SPL lists. The lists are not static and can have additions or deletions on a daily basis. Considering the many lists in play and the fact that each can change on any given day, it is essential that you receive these lists from a third party. There are reputable third parties that make it their business to monitor the various SPL lists and ensure that the data feed is up to date.

There are three key decisions you must make regarding your subscription:

1. Choose a data provider.

2. Select specific subscription lists from those available.

3. Maintain subscription lists.

1.3.1   Choose a data provider

There are multiple options for SPL content, and we encourage you to seek out the option that makes the most sense for your business. Review the following sections to help you make your decision and compare service provider offerings to your business needs. Also, ensure that they offer the data in a SAP GTS ready format.

For the purposes of demonstration in this book, all of the screenshots with content and list names are from MK Data Services, used with permission. For more information about MK Data Services, please see:

http://www.mkdataservices.com/

1.3.2 Selecting specific subscription lists

Most third parties offer a selection of lists you can subscribe to. You need to decide which lists you require and ensure that they are included. The provider may offer individual lists to choose from or may offer a bundle of lists. Either way, make sure the lists you must have are included in the agreement you make. If there is any doubt about your requirements, get outside help to assist you, such as a trade compliance consultant.

You will find a more detailed discussion in the compliance tips provided in Section 1.9. Appendix 1: SPL list types and references also provides a table of commonly used SPL lists and their abbreviations.

1.3.3 Maintenance of subscription lists

However, having a subscription service is not enough. You also need to ensure two things:

1. Daily updates to the SPL data as changes/additions are sent to you by your subscription provider.
2. A strategy for screening all of your previously released business partners against the daily changes.

Daily updates

The various sanctioned party lists are subject to change at any time and may have additions/modifications daily when the global political climate demands it. The government uses many of these lists as economic sanctions, designed to deter the behavior of another country, or perhaps stop the activities of a non-country based organization (such as drug cartels or terrorists). When global events demand a rapid response, the US government can add new entities daily as members of these groups are identified.

Sticking with US government lists as examples, you are expected to restrict activity with the listed party the day they are publicly listed (such as through a notice in the Federal Register). For example, imagine you have a customer you have dealt with for years and had no reason to suspect them of illegal activity. Unfortunately, they are in fact part of a drug cartel, and the costs/profits from their business are a way for the drug kingpins to launder their drug proceeds. The DEA realizes this, and your customer ends up listed as a sanctioned party under the Department of the Treasury OFAC rules.

You need to ask yourself:

 Does your business have the responsiveness to react to SPL list changes immediately? Imagine that the President just listed someone by Executive Order today. Will the order you have on the books shipping tomorrow to this customer be blocked?

To ensure this, you must work with your SPL data provider and ensure that they are giving you updates daily and that you are plugging those into your GTS system daily. Typically, data providers will feed you the updates through a web portal or an FTP site. This will not automatically load the change to SAP GTS; you must ensure that a system is in place to do so. Failing to be responsive could be a fatal weakness in your SPL compliance strategy.

Rescreening previously released partners (delta screenings)

Another critical action related to the daily updates is rescreening your existing customer base against the updates/additions. When you update the SPL data with the new data from your provider, this only ensures that future screenings will include this new, updated data. What about your previously screened partners? Sticking with our example from above, for the customer that is now a listed OFAC sanctioned party, what will block the delivery?

It's important to understand how SAP GTS manages screened partners and documents to make this clear. Figure 1.19 demonstrates how SAP handles a previously screened partner and any documents using that partner.

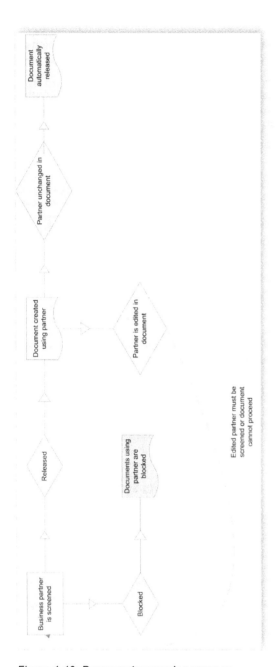

Figure 1.19: Document screening process

Once a Business Partner (BP) is released, provided it is never edited, it can be used in documents going forward without a block. Furthermore, as long as that document does not edit the partner at all, it will not even be screened (because the system notes that the partner has already been screened and released). Sticking with our example, we could have a problem if the BP was added subsequently to an SPL list after its release. This situation is illustrated in Figure 1.20.

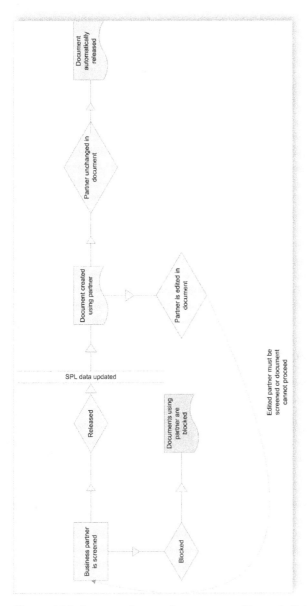

Figure 1.20: Document screening process with newly listed entity

As you can see in our example, even though we updated our SPL data, our existing customer will still be processed on a sales order without a block! How should you deal with this? You need to run delta screenings daily if you want maximum compliance and protection. A *delta screening* screens **all** of your previously released partners against the changed/updated SPL. It will only screen against SPL entries that are new or changed, since the BP was already screened against all the other SPL data previously.

In our example, this would cause our BP to be blocked since it would be screened against the new SPL data, which includes the OFAC list they were just added to. This also ensures documents using that BP will be blocked.

Performing daily updates and delta screenings ensures the highest level of compliance and protection.

1.4   TREX

With SAP NetWeaver 7.0, SAP released SAP NetWeaver Search and Classification 7.0 (*TREX*) technology. SAP GTS 7.2 and higher can make use of the technology to search and compare addresses with sanctioned party list (SPL) screening. The screening can be very performance-intensive because it searches across names, addresses, and many characters within associated fields. TREX can help make this smoother and more efficient while improving your chances of finding a close match.

TREX also provides the enhanced ability to dissect words. Standard GTS SPL functionality requires "word within word" matching. For example, "Kevin" must be found in "Kevinski." "Kevin" would not hit against "Kenvin" without TREX. TREX will allow for this kind of scrambled search, provided the total percent of letters matches. For this reason, TREX is considered a superior tool, and we recommend using it.

TREX provides the latest search technology available, which is adopted for catalog search and other features. This tool is an alternative to the main or core SPL search functionality. One of the advantages of using the TREX central engine is that you can exploit advanced features in future releases of TREX, such as TREX 7.1.

To implement TREX, you need to perform the following actions:

- ▶ Install TREX.
- ▶ If you're using TREX 7.0, you need a 32-bit processor.
- ▶ If you're using TREX 7.1, you need a 62-bit processor.
- ▶ Set up a Remote Function Call (RFC) connection between SAP GTS and TREX.
- ▶ Select required configuration settings in SAP GTS (see Section 1.2.2).
- ▶ Make a SAP GTS cockpit setting for the TREX RFC connection setup.
- ▶ Address operational considerations, such as transferring the TREX search index for SPL screening and using the central SAP NetWeaver search engine.

After the installation, TREX is assigned a logical name that is used for the RFC. You can define the RFC destination by following the menu path SAP GTS AREA MENU • SAP COMPLIANCE MANAGEMENT • SANCTIONED PARTY LIST SCREENING • MASTER DATA • GENERAL SETTINGS • COMPARISON TERMS FOR THE SANCTIONED PARTY LIST • TREX DESTINATION (see Figure 1.21).

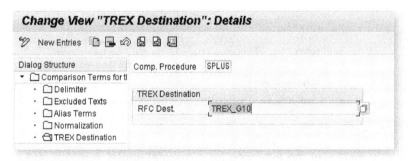

Figure 1.21: New entry for RFC destination

Within the TREX DESTINATION screen, you can maintain the RFC entry from the RFC DEST. drop-down menu. You might have several servers defined for different applications that communicate with SAP GTS, so just select the server that is configured for TREX (e.g., RFC DEST).

1.4.1 TREX configuration settings

To activate TREX, follow menu path SAP GTS AREA MENU • SAP COMPLI-
ANCE MANAGEMENT • SANCTIONED PARTY LIST SCREENING SERVICE • CON-
TROL PROCEDURE FOR ADDRESS COMPARISON (see Figure 1.22). Select the
ACTIVATE TREX check box and maintain the values in the fields SEARCH
ALGORIT. (algorithm) and MATCH RATE.

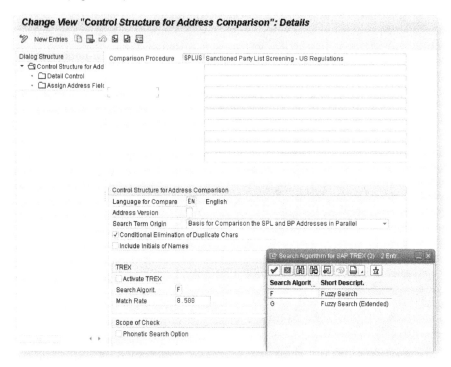

Figure 1.22: TREX activation and configuration setup

For MATCH RATE, set the tolerance for a minimal match. A match rate of
60 percent (which is represented as 6000 in the MATCH RATE field)
means that a 10-character word contains four matching letters.

Select F – FUZZY SEARCH or G – FUZZY SEARCH (EXTENDED) from the
drop-down menu for SEARCH ALGORIT. to activate the SAP TREX functionality. The search algorithm G generates more hits because it does not
have the same restrictions in the search as F does. With F, the first two
characters have to be a match. With the match rate, you can specify the
tolerance; for example, 4,000 match rate would mean that 60 percent of
the characters have to be matched in a word to be found as a hit.

SAP GTS version 11.0 changes

With SAP GTS version 11 and SAP HANA enabled, you can set up the standard SPL screening without activating TREX. We will explain the updates in detail in Chapter 3, which covers the GTS 11 release.

Operational considerations

If you have activated TREX, after you build the SPL index, you need to transfer the indices to TREX. Follow menu path SAP GTS AREA MENU • SAP COMPLIANCE MANAGEMENT • SANCTIONED PARTY LIST SCREENING • COMPARISON TERMS FOR SANCTIONED PARTY LISTS • TRANSFER COMPARISON TERMS TO TREX (see Figure 1.23). In the LEGAL REGULATION field, choose the appropriate selection from the drop-down list (in this example, it would be SPLUS). By transferring the index to TREX, the TREX search engine can use the indices for address comparison instead of the character strings. This facilitates faster searches.

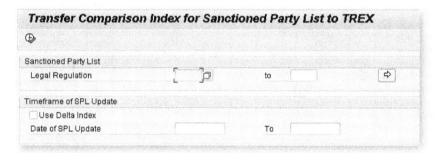

Figure 1.23: Transfer the index to TREX

The system uses the core SPL logic first and then further validates with the TREX search. The TREX search algorithm uses the match record, which looks for resemblance or similarity between the business partner search term and the SPL term. In other words, the search terms are compared based on the match record percentage defined in the configuration.

In conclusion, we would like to emphasize that we highly recommend that you use TREX. TREX will require some extra setup work—both in GTS and externally to set up the TREX hardware. However, it will give you more robust and more accurate screening results. The net result should be increased true positives and decreased false positives.

1.5 Email alerts

When you configure SAP GTS, you can set it so that users are warned when they create a partner or document that is blocked. Typically, the primary SAP ECC system (we will assume ECC is used) will display a warning message to the SAP user as displayed in Figure 1.24.

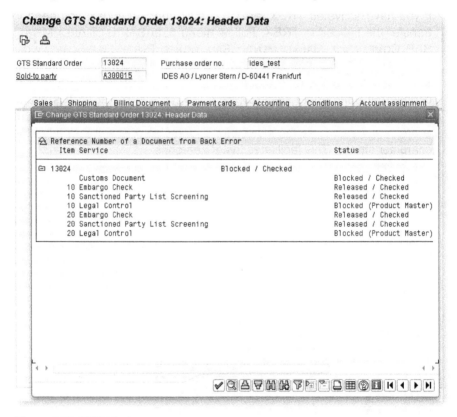

Figure 1.24: GTS block pop-up

The example in Figure 1.24 is the warning message that appears when a customer service agent enters a new sales order and GTS finds a potential match resulting in a blocked document.

SAP GTS also has the functionality to email users when it blocks a document or a business partner. This is important because the user who caused the block (e.g., by entering the order) is usually not the same user who will review/release the block. You will want these emails to go directly to the individual or group responsible for review/release of GTS blocks. See Section 1.2.1 for setup instructions.

Please see Section 1.9 of this chapter for additional compliance tips information and a suggested release/notification strategy.

1.6 Logistics – daily execution

The SPL functions in the Logistics – Daily Execution section are all accessed through the following screens. First, in the GTS main menu, select the GTS AREA MENU using transaction /SAPSLL/MENU_LEGAL (see Figure 1.25).

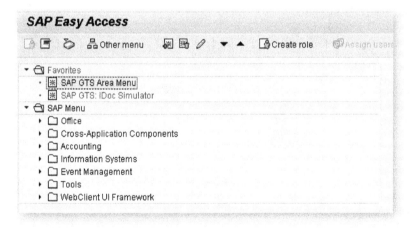

Figure 1.25 : GTS area menu

From there, you will be in what is called the Global Trade Services "Cockpit" (see Figure 1.26).

From here, select SANCTIONED PARTY LIST SCREENING, and you will see the LOGISTICS tab in Figure 1.27.

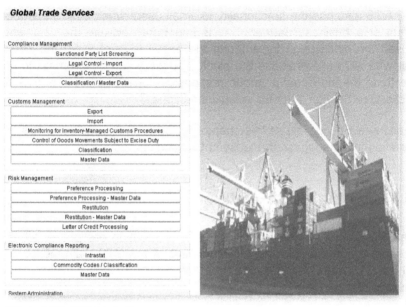

Figure 1.26: GTS cockpit

Figure 1.27: SAP compliance management SPL logistics

1.6.1   Business partner checking

Menu options

To view currently blocked partners, proceed to the screen DISPLAY BLOCKED BUSINESS PARTNERS. The menu is shown in Figure 1.28.

The following options will be available to you to narrow your search. You can hit execute without any refinements to see all blocked partners. Let's review the important fields in this section.

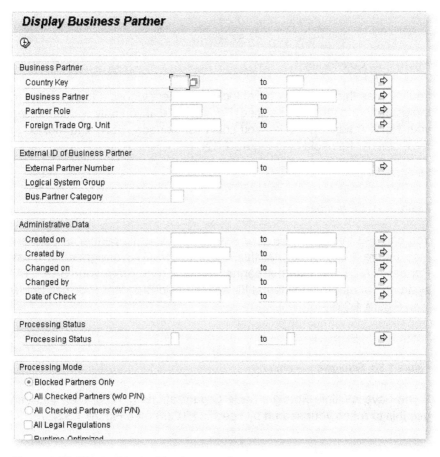

Figure 1.28: Display blocked business partner

Figure 1.29: Processing mode

Ensure that the PROCESSING MODE is set to BLOCKED PARTNERS ONLY, or you will see unblocked partners as well, which is unnecessary (see Figure 1.29).

Figure 1.30: Country key

You can use this to display only blocked partners whose addresses are in the country or countries specified. For example, if you only wanted to see your North American blocks, you could list Canada, USA, and Mexico in the COUNTRY KEY field (see Figure 1.30).

Figure 1.31: BP number

You can use this to narrow your search to a specific partner or partners (see Figure 1.31). Note that this refers to the GTS assigned Business Partner – NOT the external partner number (e.g., from your SAP ECC system). To refer to an external ID, see the field BUSINESS PARTNER below (see Figure 1.33).

Figure 1.32: Foreign trade org unit

If you have multiple Foreign Trade Organizations (FTOs), then you can use this to refine your search by specific FTO(s) (see Figure 1.32).

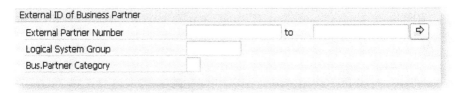

Figure 1.33: External ID of business partner

The following three fields can be ignored, unless an EXTERNAL BUSINESS PARTNER is entered. If it is entered, then the other two fields will become required fields.

EXTERNAL BUSINESS PARTNER – refers to the number from your feeder system (e.g., customer number in SAP). You can paste a list of partners in to see multiples.

LOGICAL SYSTEM GROUP – refers to your feeder system (e.g., SAP).

BUS. PARTNER CATEGORY – you cannot select multiples. They are typically either 1 (vendor) or 2 (customer), but the full list is shown in Figure 1.34.

Business Partner Category in Feeder System (1) 11 Entr...

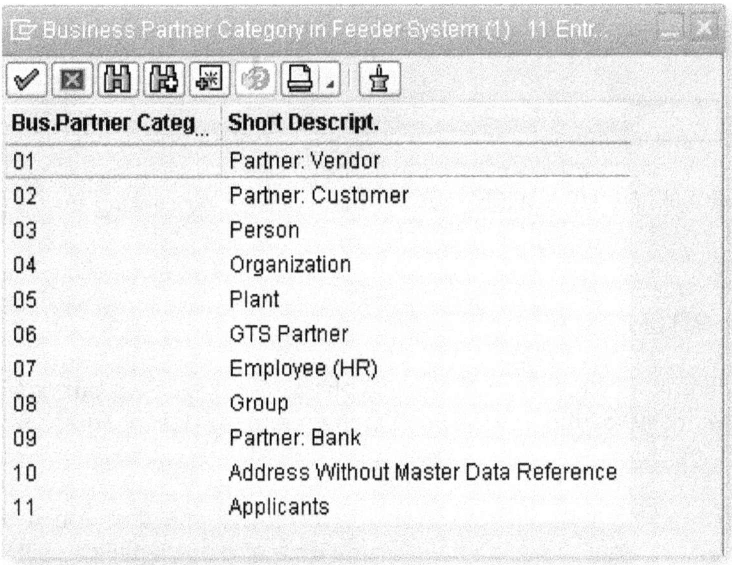

Bus.Partner Categ...	Short Descript.
01	Partner: Vendor
02	Partner: Customer
03	Person
04	Organization
05	Plant
06	GTS Partner
07	Employee (HR)
08	Group
09	Partner: Bank
10	Address Without Master Data Reference
11	Applicants

Figure 1.34: Business partner categories

Variants

As with most SAP search screens, you can save a specific set of criteria as a variant. Once your choices are made, go to Goto-variants-save as variant. After providing a name and description, click Copy Screen Assignment as shown in Figure 1.35.

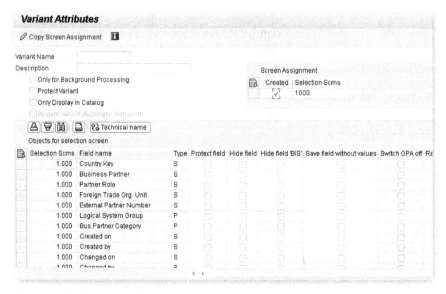

Figure 1.35: Variant attributes

The variant will now be available on the main screen by clicking on Get variant or selecting [Shift] + [F5].

Reviewing BP blocks

After selecting Execute, you will see all your currently blocked business partners (restricted by the options used in the menu, as described above) in Figure 1.36.

We recommended that you customize this layout to one that you find easy to use. You want to see all the relevant data at a quick glance, without having to scroll to the right. Here is a suggested layout shown in Figure 1.36 (but you should design one that suits your own needs):

Display Business Partner

⊕Sanctioned Party List Screening ⧉Release Partner ⬚Positive List ⬚Negative List ⬚Confirm Block ⬚On Hold 🗏 🗐 ⊕ 🗏 🗐 ⊕ ⊽ ⊽ ⊐ ⊲ 🗐 ⊤ ▦ ⁝

Blocked Business Partners

Status	LS Group	B	External Business Partner No.	Partner	L.Reg.	C	P	AddressNo.	Date of SPL Screening	Sanct Block	Validity	Created by	Created on
▧○○	ECC100G	02	3240	1470	SPL.		🔲	13586	27.01.2014 15:08:18		30.12.9999	USERRFC	27.01.2014 15:08:19
▧○○	ECC100G	02	265	1515	SPL.		🔲	13681	27.07.2014 18:13:32		04.05.2016	USERRFC	27.07.2014 18:13:33
▧○○	ECC100G	02	273	1523	SPL.		🔲	13689	27.07.2014 18:13:35		04.05.2016	USERRFC	27.07.2014 18:13:36
▧○○	ECC100G	02	281	1524	SPL.		🔲	13690	27.07.2014 18:13:38		30.12.9999	USERRFC	27.07.2014 18:13:38
▧○○	ECC100G	02	483	1533	SPL.		🔲	13699	27.07.2014 18:13:39		29.12.9999	USERRFC	27.07.2014 18:13:39
▧○○	ECC100G	02	505	1536	SPL.		🔲	13702	27.07.2014 18:13:40		29.12.9999	USERRFC	27.07.2014 18:13:40
▧○○	ECC100G	02	521	1549	SPL.		🔲	13715	27.07.2014 18:13:44		30.12.9999	USERRFC	27.07.2014 18:13:44
▧○○	ECC100G	02	539	1555	SPL.		🔲	13721	27.07.2014 18:13:47		29.12.9999	USERRFC	27.07.2014 18:13:47
▧○○	ECC100G	02	555	1564	SPL.		🔲	13730	27.07.2014 18:13:49		29.12.9999	USERRFC	27.07.2014 18:13:49
▧○○	ECC100G	02	559	1568	SPL.		🔲	13734	27.07.2014 18:13:50		30.12.9999	USERRFC	27.07.2014 18:13:51
▧○○	ECC100G	02	573	1576	SPL		🔲	13742	27.07.2014 18:13:53		29.12.9999	USERRFC	27.07.2014 18:13:53
▧○○	ECC100G	02	1172	1606	SPL.		🔲	13772	27.07.2014 18:14:03		29.12.9999	USERRFC	27.07.2014 18:14:03
▧○○	ECC100G	02	1330	1633	SPL.		🔲	13799	27.07.2014 18:14:11		29.12.9999	USERRFC	27.07.2014 18:14:11
▧○○	ECC100G	02	1948	1675	SPL.		🔲	13841	27.07.2014 18:14:26		29.12.9999	USERRFC	27.07.2014 18:14:26
▧○○	ECC100G	02	2402	1718	SPL.		🔲	13884	27.07.2014 18:14:39		30.12.9999	USERRFC	27.07.2014 18:14:40
▧○○	ECC100G	02	3065	1771	SPL.		🔲	13937	27.07.2014 18:14:57		29.12.9999	USERRFC	27.07.2014 18:14:58
▧○○	ECC100G	02	3075	1781	SPL.		🔲	13947	27.07.2014 18:15:01		30.12.9999	USERRFC	27.07.2014 18:15:01
▧○○	ECC100G	02	3078	1784	SPL.		🔲	13950	27.07.2014 18:15:02		29.12.9999	USERRFC	27.07.2014 18:15:02
▧○○	ECC100G	02	3187	1799	SPL.		🔲	13966	27.07.2014 18:15:07		30.12.9999	USERRFC	27.07.2014 18:15:07
▧○○	ECC100G	02	3550	1902	SPL.		🔲	14066	27.07.2014 18:15:44		30.12.9999	USERRFC	27.07.2014 18:15:44
▧○○	ECC100G	02	3751	1922	SPL.		🔲	14088	27.07.2014 18:15:50		30.12.9999	USERRFC	27.07.2014 18:15:50
▧○○	ECC100G	02	3755	1923	SPL.		🔲	14089	27.07.2014 18:15:50		30.12.9999	USERRFC	27.07.2014 18:15:50
▧○○	ECC100G	02	3997	1957	SPL		🔲	14123	27.07.2014 18:16:00		29.12.9999	USERRFC	27.07.2014 18:16:00
▧○○	ECC100G	02	4060	1965	SPL.		🔲	14131	27.07.2014 18:16:03		30.12.9999	USERRFC	27.07.2014 18:16:03
▧○○	ECC100G	02	8888	2066	RPI		🔲	14232	27.07.2014 18:16:34		29.12.9999	USERRFC	27.07.2014 18:16:34

Figure 1.36: Blocked business partners

To change the layout, simply click on the CHANGE LAYOUT button, which looks like a spreadsheet ▦. Assign columns to be hidden or shown and rearrange the order as desired. Figure 1.37 displays suggested settings, but you can tailor the view however you wish.

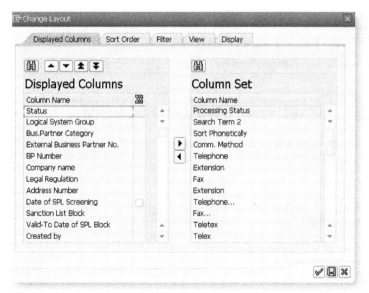

Figure 1.37: Suggested layout

Save your layout changes

Remember to save your changes as a layout, or you will have to do this the next time you view the list (see Figure 1.38)!

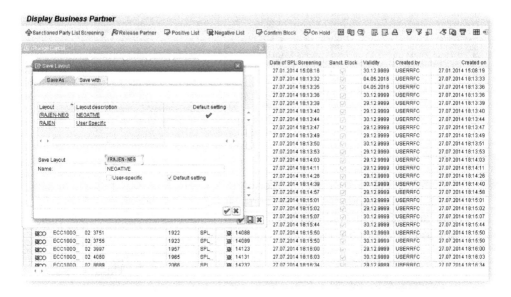

Figure 1.38: Save layout changes for future use

To review the details of the block, highlight the partner in question and click on DETAILED ANALYSIS, which looks like a puzzle piece.

In Figure 1.39, you can see a detailed analysis of a block called the *SPL Audit Trail*. Let's take a closer look at the elements on this screen.

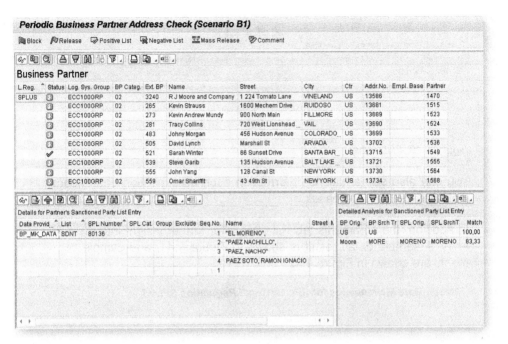

Figure 1.39: SPL audit trail

Audit Trail Screen

BUSINESS PARTNER: This is your business partner from SAP ECC or another source.

SPL ENTRIES: These are the (one or more) SPL entities that have been deemed a "match" against your business partner, as per the configuration settings. You can see the SPL List they belong to and basic address information. To see more detail, click on DISPLAY SPL DATA as described in Figure 1.40.

MATCHED TERMS: These are the actual words that caused the match for you to review.

You can click on the DISPLAY SPL DATA button 🖨 to see more detail on any specific SPL Entry (see Figure 1.40).

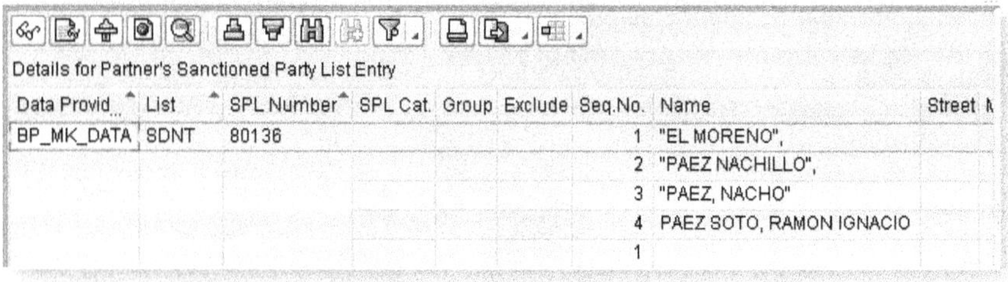

Data Provid...	List	SPL Number	SPL Cat.	Group	Exclude	Seq.No.	Name	Street N
BP_MK_DATA	SDNT	80136				1	"EL MORENO",	
						2	"PAEZ NACHILLO",	
						3	"PAEZ, NACHO"	
						4	PAEZ SOTO, RAMON IGNACIO	
						1		

Figure 1.40: SPL entity

You can also see additional information such as expiration dates, complete names, and addresses.

In addition, the comments tab will often offer further insight into the SPL entry. A sample detail result is shown in Figure 1.41, and sample comments are shown in Figure 1.42.

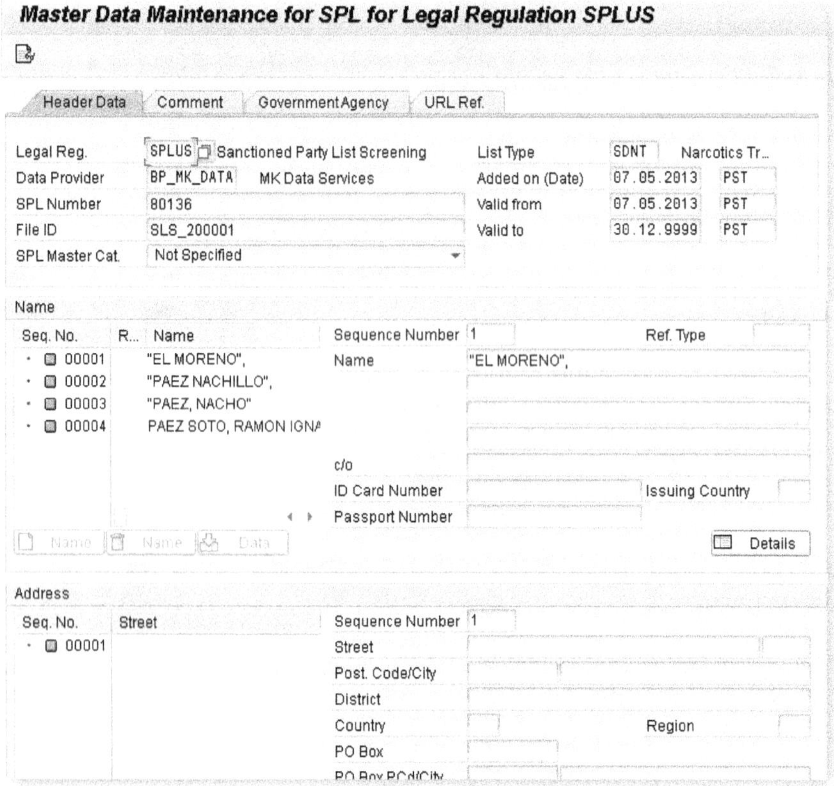

Figure 1.41: SPL entity details

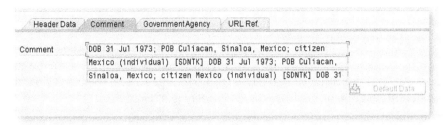

Figure 1.42: Comments/details specific to SPL entity

Lastly, if your SPL data provider offers it, you may be able to launch its website from here for further information. An example from MK Data Services is shown in Figure 1.43.

Figure 1.43: URL reference tied to SPL entity

Based on the review above, you must now decide whether to release your business partner. Click BACK ⌖ to return to the results screen and make your decision. You cannot execute your decision in the audit trail screen.

Releasing business partners

As explained, you must exit the detailed analysis/audit trail to effect a release decision. This is done primarily in the BLOCKED BUSINESS PART-NERS results screen. From this screen, you have the ability to perform several functions. In the sections that follow, we will provide a quick summary of the functions, as well as a more in depth review of the re-lease process (if you choose that function). Keep in mind that, for all of the options, you must first highlight the partner in question before you select your function option.

Functions

SANCTIONED PARTY LIST SCREENING: Triggers a fresh screening of the partner against the current SPL lists. This is useful if you have reason to believe that the SPL lists have changed and a fresh screening will yield a different result (e.g., perhaps the SPL entity is expired now).

RELEASE PARTNER: Releases the business partner and allows it to be used in documents.

POSITIVE LIST: Places the partner on the positive list and allows it to be used in documents.

NEGATIVE LIST: Places the partner on the negative list and prevents its use in documents.

CONFIRM BLOCK: Confirms that the block is valid but will not place it on the negative list. Future users will be able to see this confirmation. It will not be usable in documents.

ON HOLD: Places the partner on hold, and future users will see that it is in a hold status. This is useful if you want to prevent another user from accidentally releasing the partner while you do further research. The partner will not be usable in documents.

As RELEASE PARTNER is the likely outcome in the majority cases, we cover it in further detail below.

Release Partner

If you have made the decision to release the business partner, the typical process is as follows. From the BLOCKED BUSINESS PARTNERS results screen, highlight the partner in question and click on the RELEASE PARTNER button as shown in Figure 1.44. This can be done for more than one partner at a time by holding down Ctrl or Shift as you select the partners.

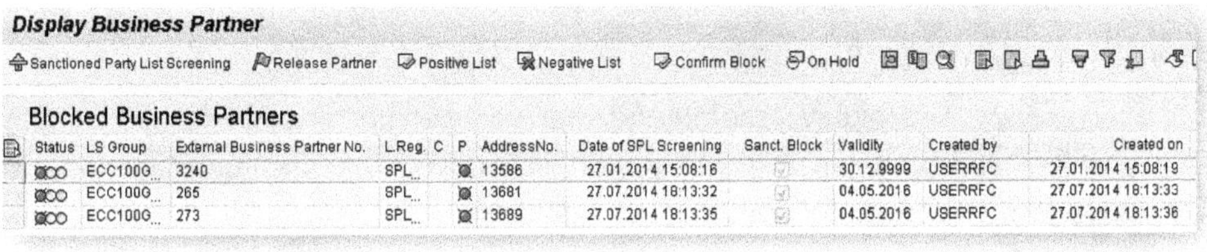

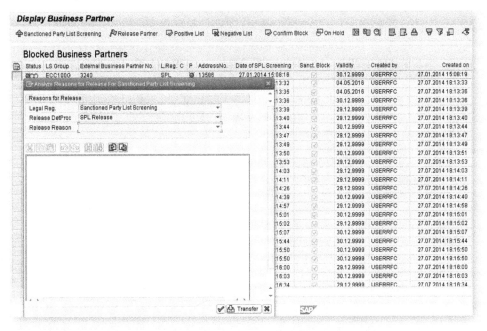

Figure 1.44: Blocked business partner display

Once you click on RELEASE PARTNER, you will go to a screen called the ANALYZE REASONS FOR RELEASE FOR SANCTIONED PARTY LIST SCREENING dialogue. You can see this important pop-up menu in Figure 1.45.

Figure 1.45: Analyze reasons for release for SPL entry

On this screen, you can do two things to record the reason for release. The first is to click on the RELEASE REASON drop-down menu. This will bring up the various reasons you have assigned as options in configuration. There is no default or system-provided list of reasons; you must assign the reasons that make sense for your business.

Reasons for release

 We highly recommend that you set up reasons for release, as this will accomplish several things items important for compliance, including:

▶ It forces the user to put some thought into why exactly they are releasing the entity.

▶ It provides an audit trail, and you can run reports showing why partners were released.

▶ It show any future external auditor that thought (and due diligence) went into the release decision.

Secondly, you can enter text describing your reason for release. We recommend doing so when the release required unusual research, or if you fear the release could be misinterpreted for any reason If you type a narrative here, ensure that you save it by selecting ⛁ Transfer before you select CONTINUE ✅.

See Section 1.2.6 for a review of how to set up reasons for release and some suggested reasons.

Once you select CONTINUE, your partner is released and will no longer show in the results screen. Don't worry; if you ever accidentally release the wrong one, you can re-block them! To do that, you would return to the menu for DISPLAY BLOCKED BUSINESS PARTNERS and check off ALL CHECKED PARTNERS as shown in Figure 1.46. Make sure that you enter your business partner number, or you will be essentially returning all of your business partners back in the results screen!

Figure 1.46: Processing mode selection

1.6.2 Document checking

Menu options

To view currently blocked documents, proceed to the screen MANUALLY RELEASE BLOCKED DOCUMENTS. There is also a screen titled DISPLAY BLOCKED DOCUMENTS, however it lacks a release mechanism. This is useful if you want to give some users display access, but not the ability to release. Since most users want to release at the same time as they review, we are showing only the screen where you can do both: MANUALLY RELEASE BLOCKED DOCUMENTS.

Figure 1.47 shows the menu screen before you get to the results.

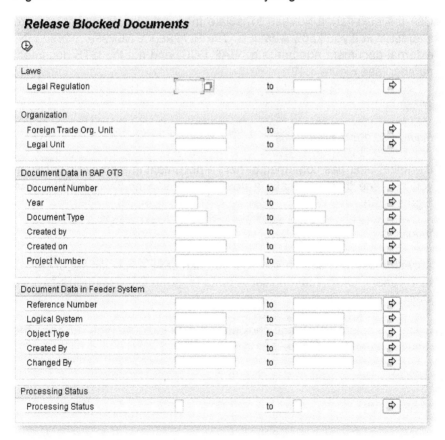

Figure 1.47 Release blocked document menu

The following options will be available to you to narrow your search. You can hit execute without any refinements to see all blocked partners. A discussion of important fields follows.

Figure 1.48: Foreign trade org. unit

Use FOREIGN TRADE ORG. UNIT to filter your results by FTO, such as a company division or country unit (see Figure 1.48).

Figure 1.49: Reference number

Use the REFERENCE NUMBER to isolate the particular document you are interested in if you know what it is. The REFERENCE NUMBER refers to the external document number (e.g., SAP ECC) and not the GTS document number (see Figure 1.49).

Figure 1.50: Processing status

If another user has confirmed or held a document in a previous decision, you can see that and make a next step or second-level decision (see Figure 1.50).

VARIANTS

As with most SAP search screens, you can save a specific set of criteria as a variant. Once your choices are made, go to GOTO-VARIANTS-SAVE AS VARIANT.

Once you select your menu choices and click EXECUTE, you will go to the results screen (see Figure 1.51).

SPL Screening: Release Blocked Documents

Blocked Documents with Item Data

Ref. No.	Log.System	SPL Screen	Embargo	Control	Restitutn	Lett.Cred.	Prog Sts	Haz.Subst	FT.Org.	Item	SPL Screen	Embargo	Control	Restitutn	Lett.Cred.	Prog Sts	Haz.Subst	Product No	Ctry of PL	Dep
13426	T90CLNT090								FTO3000	20								MEMORY1	US	US
13940	ECCCLNT110								FTO3000	10										
13942									FTO_US3000	10								R-1141	US	U9
14061	ECCCLNT100								FTO_US3000	10								Z6TS-N3	US	US
14076									FTO_US3000	10								Z6TS-N3	US	US
14081									FTO_US3000	10								X1 BALAST	US	US
14082									FTO_US3000	10								X1 BALAST	US	US
14085									FTO_US3000	10								X1 BALAST	US	US
14086									FTO_US3000	10								01-9930	US	US
									FTO_US3000	20								01-9931	US	US
14089									FTO_US3000	10								01-9930	US	US
14104									FTO_US3000	10								X1 BALAST	US	US
14105									FTO_US3000	10								X1 BALAST	US	US
14112									FTO_US3000	10								Z6TS-N4	US	US
5111111									FTO_US3000	10								Z6TS-N3	US	US
80016266	T90CLNT090								FTO3000	10								GTS-30003	US	US
80016780	ECCCLNT110								FTO_US3000	10								R-1141	US	U9
90038102	T90CLNT090								FTO3000	10								MEMORY1	US	US
90038110									FTO3000	10								GTS-30003	US	US
90038111									FTO3000	10								MEMORY1	US	US
4151511110									FTO001	10								T-M15A10	US	DE
									FTO001	20								T-M15B10	US	DE
									FTO001	30								T-M15C10	US	DE
									FTO001	40								T-M15D10	US	DE

Figure 1.51: Release blocked documents results

In the next section, we will discuss the process for reviewing and then releasing the documents (if appropriate).

Reviewing document blocks and releasing

Within the results screen, you can analyze the reason for the block by clicking on the DETAILED ANALYSIS button 🖳. This will show you an audit trail for the block, the same as it would in reviewing a blocked partner. However, unlike a BP review, the results can look different here, depending on the status of the partner used in the document.

This audit can have two results:

1. Show the SPL entry (or entries) that the document is blocked against (see Figure 1.52).

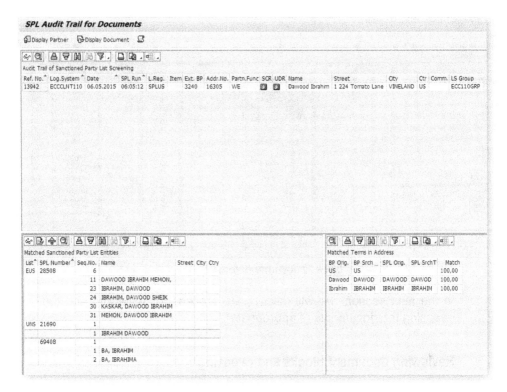

Figure 1.52: SPL audit trail for document

2. Not show anything in the MATCHED SANCTIONED PARTY LIST ENTITIES SECTION (see Figure 1.53).

Each situation must be handled differently:

Situation 1 – SPL entity shown in detailed analysis screen:

This typically occurs when the document itself has been checked using the system's configured "match logic." For example, if the business partner used in an order or delivery was not blocked, but then it was edited subsequently in the delivery, it could cause a document block. In these cases, you can see the results of the screening and review the audit details of the SPL block.

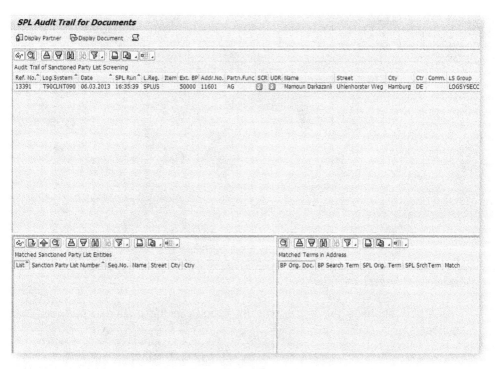

Figure 1.53: SPL audit trail without SPL entity

When this occurs, you can release the document by clicking on the green arrow to go back to the results screen. Back in the results screen, you can either click the green flag CANCEL SPL BLOCK 📕, which will cancel the SPL block, or you can do a fresh SPL screening using the PERFORM SPL SCREENING button 🖨.

The CANCEL SPL BLOCK option is quicker and will immediately take you to the reason for release screen (see Figure 1.54).

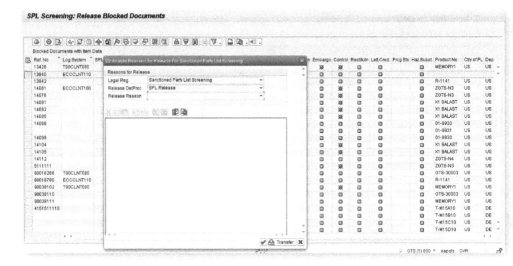

Figure 1.54: Reason for release

This report behaves the same was as it does in the business partner section.

The PERFORM SPL SCREENING option is longer, and takes you through a fresh screening of the partner; however, it also forces you to double-check the reason for the release. The danger of CANCEL SPL BLOCK is that you need to already have reviewed the audit of the block and be 100 percent confident that this document should be released. Use this only if you are confident that you have selected the correct document. If there are multiple documents blocked, and you believe there is a risk of can-celling the block on the wrong document, then use the fresh SPL screen-ing option. With this option, you will have the choice to release the doc-ument while looking at the audit trail, ensuring that you are releasing the correct document.

Furthermore, if the document has sat blocked for a length of time, it is a good idea to run the SPL screening again in case it now matches a new SPL entity (assuming you are doing regular updates to the SPL data-base).

Situation 2 – No SPL entity shown in detailed analysis screen:

This occurs when the document is blocked as a result of a partner in that document already being blocked. You will not see the detailed audit trail for the block since the document was not truly audited—as soon as the partner was blocked, the document was also blocked. In this case, you need to release the partner first. This is done through the regular RE-LEASE BLOCKED PARTNER function described in Section 1.6.1.

Once the partner is released, click on the RECHECK button 🔄 , and the document will release. Save the result and the document is no longer blocked.

Note that this will happen if the partner is blocked and not released yet, or if the partner is on the negative list (see Section 1.6.3).

1.6.3   Positive and negative lists

Positive lists and negative lists remove the business partners listed from future checks. The *positive lists* ensure that the partner can always be used in documents without further blocks. The *negative lists* ensure that the partner stays blocked and will not be automatically rechecked. Until a user manually releases the partner from the negative list, all documents containing this partner will block. As you can guess, the positive list creates a large compliance risk and must only be used in the case of 100 percent guaranteed, safe entities that could not possibly be listed. We recommend great care and caution if you decide to use this function.

There are four key functions related to the positive and negative lists:

1.   Check positive list business partner address.

2.   Check negative list business partner address.

3.   Display positive list business partner.

4.   Display negative list business partner.

Let's now walk through the two negative list functions in detail, which you are more likely to use than the positive list.

Please note that this area is intended for reviewing and rechecking listed entities. How an entity becomes listed is covered in Section 1.6.1. If the user placed a BP on one of these two lists at the time of release, then this section is where you can review them or recheck them to potentially remove them from the list.

Display negative list business partner

The screen in Figure 1.55 is used to view the partners that have been placed on the negative list. You can leave all of options wide open, or you can narrow the search by multiple fields, such as date of SPL screening or BP number.

Figure 1.55: Display negative list menu

After you hit execute, you will be presented with the list of currently listed partners (see Figure 1.56).

Display Business Partner

Business Partners on the Negative List

Status	LS Group	External Business Partner No.	L.Reg.	C	P	AddressNo.	Date of SPL Screening	Sanct. Block	Validity	Created by	Created on	Changed by	Changed on	Flagged o
▣○	LOG6YSE	3755	SPL		▣	11371	19.12.2011 11:42:41	▢	30.12.9999	USERRFC	10.11.2011 13:35:44	JEFF	19.12.2011 11:42:41	
▣○	LOG6YSE	300281	SPL	▣	▣	11954	05.08.2014 16:21:49	✓		USERRFC	10.11.2011 13:39:10	REBECCA	05.08.2014 16:21:49	
▣○	LOG6YSE	3187	SPL		▣	11248	03.08.2012 12:59:04	▢		USERRFC	10.11.2011 13:34:58	RAJESH	03.08.2012 12:59:04	

Figure 1.56: Display negative list results

There is nothing more to be done on this screen. If you want to review the reason for a partners' listing, or take them off the negative list, you need to go to the next function.

Check negative list business partner address

On this screen, you can re-screen a partner on the negative list. This will allow you to either leave it on the list or release it. This is typically done for two reasons:

1. A review of the listed party, either as part of a periodic review, or because you have reason to believe they should no longer be blocked.

2. A review of the decision to list a party, by a higher-level user. For example, a first-level review may have resulted in a negative listing, and that user's manager is now reviewing that decision as part of a second-level review. See Section 1.9 for a more detailed discussion of first- and second-level reviews.

We recommend that you specify a specific business partner on this screen (see Figure 1.57); otherwise, you will cause all listed partners to be reviewed. Note that you will also have to specify the LOGICAL SYSTEM GROUP and the BUS. PARTNER CATEGORY.

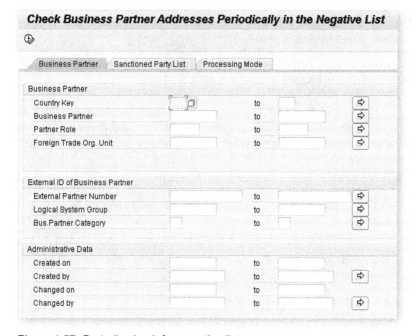

Figure 1.57: Periodic check for negative list menu

After you hit execute, you will be taken to a detailed analysis/audit trail screen to view the results of the partner's SPL screening (see Figure 1.58).

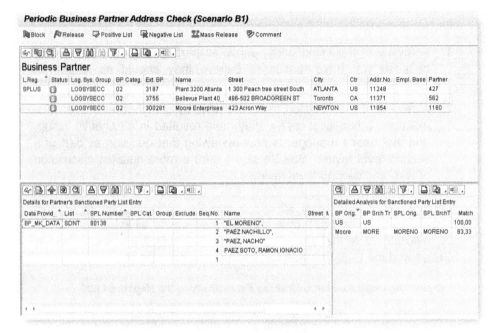

Figure 1.58: Negative list periodic check results

On this screen, you have several choices. These choices are similar to those when you initially screen a business partner; however, there are fewer options since you are dealing with a partner on the negative list. Note that, after you make your decision and click the appropriate button, you will have to select SAVE to leave this screen.

▶ BLOCK: This will take the partner off the negative list but leave it blocked.

▶ RELEASE: This will remove the partner from the negative list, and it is no longer blocked.

▶ POSITIVE LIST: This will move the partner from the negative list to the positive list.

▶ NEGATIVE LIST: This will return the partner to the negative list.

▶ MASS RELEASE: This will release all partners if you selected multiple ones on the menu screen.

1.6.4 Check external addresses

SAP GTS's most common use is in real-time communication with an ERP, typically SAP ECC.) This is the ideal situation for compliance because it ensures real-time blocking and ongoing checking of partners and documents. However, the reality is that not all of the organization's operating entities will be on the same platform, and for at least a limited time, these parts of the company may not have real-time communication with GTS.

In those cases, SAP GTS can still help using the CHECK EXTERNAL ADDRESSES (OFFLINE) functionality.

This part of the system allows for uploading an XML file, which will be checked against the SPL lists in SAP GTS. This is typically done with a customer list or a vendor list extracted from a system that is not linked to SAP GTS. These checks can be done as often as desired. Next, we will review how to run a check and go through the steps. For the purposes of the example, we will use a customer list.

The first step is to put the customer list into the required XML format. This is a template that is available to any SAP GTS user. The template is explained in APPLICATION HELP, under XML STRUCTURE FOR ADDRESS DATA IN SANCTIONED PARTY LIST SCREENING. Once you have populated the data, you need to save it as an .xml file.

You only need to worry about the fields that you set up as significant in configuration. For example, if you do not compare telephone numbers in your SPL checks, then there is no need to populate that in the spreadsheet.

Next, go to the CHECK EXTERNAL ADDRESS (OFFLINE) screen (see Figure 1.59).

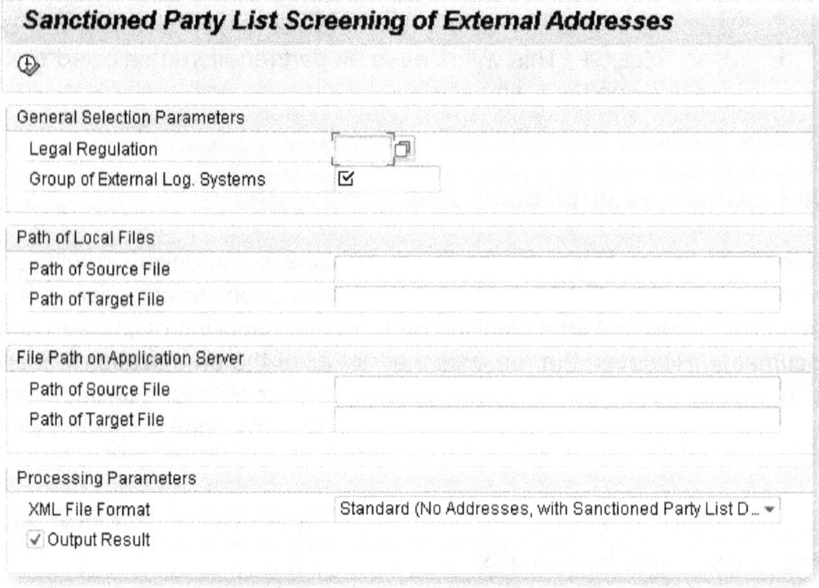

Sanctioned Party List Screening of External Addresses

General Selection Parameters	
Legal Regulation	
Group of External Log. Systems	☑

Path of Local Files	
Path of Source File	
Path of Target File	

File Path on Application Server	
Path of Source File	
Path of Target File	

Processing Parameters	
XML File Format	Standard (No Addresses, with Sanctioned Party List D... ▾
☑ Output Result	

Figure 1.59: Check external address screening

There are a few choices to consider before you click on execute:

1. LEGAL REGULATION: Select the SPL legal regulation you normally use, unless you have built a specially configured one specifically for offline screenings.

2. GROUP OF EXTERNAL LOG. SYSTEMS: You will need to create a new group for external screenings that differentiates it from the systems that are linked to SAP GTS.

3. PATH OF SOURCE FILE (LOCAL): This is a browse function similar to those used in Windows-based software. Use it to browse your local files (e.g., the "C" drive on your computer) and find the file containing the partners you want to screen.

4. PATH OF TARGET FILE (LOCAL): This is also a browse function, and you can use it to select the location of the results file (the file that shows the results of the screening, including which partners are "blocked" and which are not).

5. PATH OF SOURCE FILE (APPLICATION SERVER): This works the same as the local file version, except it means that you are looking for your file on a network server.

6. PATH OF TARGET FILE (APPLICATION SERVER): This works the same as the local file version, except it means you are saving your results file on a network server.

7. XML FILE FORMAT: There are a few options available here; experiment with each to determine your preferred layout.

8. Once you have made your selections, click EXECUTE to create a file in the target location you selected. This file will show which of the customers is considered a match "blocked" and which are not considered a match "released."

1.6.5   Audit trail reporting

The audit trail section of SPL provides detailed and historical analysis of the SPL screenings that have been done in SAP GTS. It is a way to view screening results and user decisions. It is broken into three key categories: business partners, documents, and external addresses. As the menu interface for each category is a little different, we will discuss them separately. The results of the audit trail report look nearly identical for each.

Once you have the results of the audit trail report, we recommended building a customized layout (see Section 1.6.1 for a discussion on building a new layout).

The results of the audit trail can either be reviewed in SAP GTS or exported to Excel. The results will tell you what was the result of the screening (block or not block), and in the cases of blocks, will actually show you the SPL entity or entities that were matched, resulting in a block. Figure 1.60 shows a sample layout.

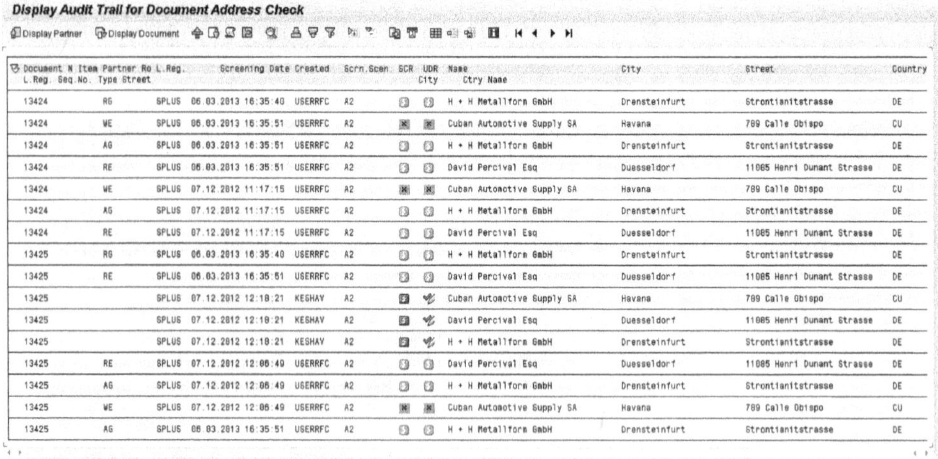

Display Audit Trail for Document Address Check

Document	N Item	Partner Ro	L.Reg.	Screening Date	Created	Scrn.Scen	SCR	UDR	Name	City	Street	Country
13424		RG	SPLUS	06.03.2013 16:35:40	USERRFC	A2			H + H Metallform GmbH	Drensteinfurt	Strontianitstrasse	DE
13424		WE	SPLUS	06.03.2013 16:35:51	USERRFC	A2			Cuban Automotive Supply SA	Havana	789 Calle Obispo	CU
13424		AG	SPLUS	06.03.2013 16:35:51	USERRFC	A2			H + H Metallform GmbH	Drensteinfurt	Strontianitstrasse	DE
13424		RE	SPLUS	06.03.2013 16:35:51	USERRFC	A2			David Percival Esq	Duesseldorf	11085 Henri Dunant Strasse	DE
13424		WE	SPLUS	07.12.2012 11:17:15	USERRFC	A2			Cuban Automotive Supply SA	Havana	789 Calle Obispo	CU
13424		AG	SPLUS	07.12.2012 11:17:15	USERRFC	A2			H + H Metallform GmbH	Drensteinfurt	Strontianitstrasse	DE
13424		RE	SPLUS	07.12.2012 11:17:15	USERRFC	A2			David Percival Esq	Duesseldorf	11085 Henri Dunant Strasse	DE
13425		RG	SPLUS	06.03.2013 16:35:40	USERRFC	A2			H + H Metallform GmbH	Drensteinfurt	Strontianitstrasse	DE
13425		RE	SPLUS	06.03.2013 16:35:51	USERRFC	A2			David Percival Esq	Duesseldorf	11085 Henri Dunant Strasse	DE
13425			SPLUS	07.12.2012 12:18:21	KESHAV	A2			Cuban Automotive Supply SA	Havana	789 Calle Obispo	CU
13425			SPLUS	07.12.2012 12:18:21	KESHAV	A2			David Percival Esq	Duesseldorf	11085 Henri Dunant Strasse	DE
13425			SPLUS	07.12.2012 12:18:21	KESHAV	A2			H + H Metallform GmbH	Drensteinfurt	Strontianitstrasse	DE
13425		RE	SPLUS	07.12.2012 12:06:49	USERRFC	A2			David Percival Esq	Duesseldorf	11085 Henri Dunant Strasse	DE
13425		AG	SPLUS	07.12.2012 12:06:49	USERRFC	A2			H + H Metallform GmbH	Drensteinfurt	Strontianitstrasse	DE
13425		WE	SPLUS	07.12.2012 12:06:49	USERRFC	A2			Cuban Automotive Supply SA	Havana	789 Calle Obispo	CU
13425		AG	SPLUS	06.03.2013 16:35:51	USERRFC	A2			H + H Metallform GmbH	Drensteinfurt	Strontianitstrasse	DE

Figure 1.60: Audit trail for documents

Audit trail for business partners

The menu for this function allows you to narrow your search using various options. Some of the key options include:

- COUNTRY KEY: Use this option to view the audit trail of all partners in a specific country. You may wish to do this periodically for high-risk countries.
- BP NUMBER: Use this option to narrow your search to a specific or multiple specific BPs.
- FOREIGN TRADE ORG. UNIT: If you have multiple organizations in play, this option allows you to review them separately.
- EXTERNAL PARTNER NUMBER**:** This option is the same as the BP number, except it uses your feeder system's number instead of the SAP GTS assigned number. Note if you use this option you must also specify the LOGICAL SYSTEM GROUP and BP CATEGORY.
- CREATED/CHANGED/DATE OF CHECK: Use this string of fields to review specific date ranges.
- PROCESSING STATUS: This option is a great way to perform second-level reviews of partners that have been placed on hold or confirmed as blocked. See Section 1.6.1 for a detailed discussion of this process.

Make sure you narrow your search

You must narrow your search in some way. Otherwise, the results will be so large that the system will either take an extremely long time to process or will outright fail!

Purpose of "On Hold"

Many users wonder why they would use the "on hold" function instead of just leaving the partner blocked; here's why! It makes for a much cleaner audit trail and it also allows a level two user (see Section 1.9.4) to easily pull up all of the matches a level one user was unable to resolve.

Audit trail for documents

Similar to AUDIT TRAIL FOR BUSINESS PARTNERS, with documents you have options to narrow your search. Some of the key options are:

▶ DATE OF SPL SCREENING: Use this option to narrow the search to a specific date range.

▶ OUTCOME OF SYSTEM CHECK: Use this option to only view screenings that resulted in a specific result. Typically, you would search only documents that were blocked by the system.

▶ OUTCOME OF USER CHECK: Use this option to only search documents that have had a user decision made for them, such as a release. This could be used to review all the documents that users have released, as an audit or second-level review.

▶ REFERENCE NUMBER: This means the external document number, e.g., an order number from SAP ECC.

Audit trail for external addresses

The options for this audit trail report are similar to the other two:

- ▶ DATE OF SPL SCREENING: Use this option to narrow the search to a specific date range. For example, if you uploaded an Excel spreadsheet, you would input the date you did that screening.

- ▶ OUTCOME OF SYSTEM CHECK: Use this option to only view screenings that resulted in a specific result. Note that even though GTS cannot truly block an external address, it will consider all SPL matches to be a "block" for this purpose.

- ▶ EXTERNAL PARTNER NUMBER: Refers to the address number that was contained in the XML file when it was loaded.

1.7 Master data

1.7.1 Maintain sanctioned party lists

Assuming you have gone with the recommended approach of using a subscription service for your SPL lists, this screen will really only be used for one purpose: to create and maintain a company-controlled SPL list.

The purpose of this list is to allow you to block partners that are not actually listed on any published SPL lists. Your company can have many reasons to use this function: a customer who failed to pay you, and you want to ensure they never get product again. Perhaps a vendor engaged in unethical behavior, not serious enough to be listed as a government SPL, but serious enough for you to discontinue all business with them. Or perhaps, a true SPL entry from a list you chose not to subscribe to. As discussed in compliance tips, there are many SPL lists, and you may not subscribe to all of them. In that case, you may find some entities on those other lists you choose to block, and this is a way to get them into your system manually.

For obvious reasons, access to this function should be strictly limited.

1.7.2 Display overview list

Display overview list is a way to review your populated SPL lists. This is a display only function, and as such, access to it can be shared with most users.

Users are able to call up all populated SPL entries and narrow the search using several options. The reasons why a user may wish to do so are varied, including to double check the accuracy of subscription data or as part of routine audits. The menu is shown in Figure 1.61. Some of the menu options are:

▶ TYPE OF LIST: Search only certain lists if desired, such as a particular Department of the Treasury Specially Designated National List.

▶ VALIDITY DATES: Narrow your search to only currently valid entries by limiting the validity date to the present and future.

▶ CHANGED/CREATED ON: If, for example, this was a subscription data audit, this option would allow you to view only those SPL entries that were created or updated in a certain date range so that you are not reviewing any that have been previously audited.

Display Sanctioned Party Lists

Sanctioned Party List			
Legal Regulation		to	⇨
Type of List		to	⇨
Data Provider		to	⇨
SPL Number		to	⇨
Country Key		to	⇨
SPL Master Category		to	⇨

Validity Data			
Valid from		to	⇨
Valid to		to	⇨

Administrative Data			
Created on		to	⇨
Changed on		to	⇨
Created by		to	⇨
Changed by		to	⇨

Processing Mode
☐ Include Deletion Inds

Figure 1.61: Display sanctioned party lists

1.7.3 Comparison terms

Comparison terms are the indexing function for GTS SPL searches. In theory, the searches can be run without these terms being up to date, but realistically, it will slow the system down and may even result in inaccurate searches. To ensure accurate and timely results, comparison terms must be run any time a change is made relevant to them. There are two general categories of terms, SPL and BP (see Figure 1.62).

Use scripts for automatic term generation

 While comparison terms can be generated manually using the cockpit, we recommend that you run them as a script automatically. Running the script each evening during off hours makes the most sense. Leaving it up to a user (manual process) puts your organization at risk if that user ever forgets or is unable to perform the function. The result would be that your data is not current and is missing up-to-date changes and/or additions.

Comparison terms for sanctioned party lists

After every change to SPL content (i.e., an update from the subscription provider), run GENERATE COMPARISON TERMS.

After this has run, you must also run AGGREGATE COMPARISON TERMS.

Note that if you have TREX active, you must also run a third function called TRANSFER COMPARISON TERMS TO TREX.

Comparison terms for business partners

After every change to BP data (e.g., new or changed BPs from SAP ECC), you must run GENERATE COMPARISON TERMS.

Figure 1.62: Comparison terms functions

1.7.4 Control settings for comparison terms

General settings

SPL master data requires you to set up the control settings for the con-figured search terms. You can do this using transaction /SAPSLL/MENU_LEGAL or following menu path SAP GRC GTS AREA MENU • SAP COMPLIANCE MANAGEMENT • SANCTIONED PARTY LIST SCREEN-ING • MASTER DATA • CONTROL SETTINGS FOR COMPARISON TERMS • GEN-ERAL SETTINGS (see Figure 1.63).

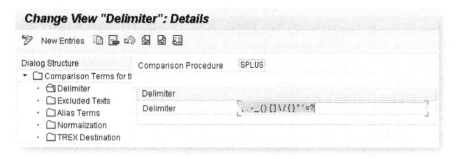

Figure 1.63 General settings

When you click GENERAL SETTINGS under CONTROL SETTINGS FOR COMPARISON TERMS, there are subfolders that contain the following fields:

▶ DELIMITER: Lists all special characters, including numbers the content file might have (e.g., hyphens, commas, or quotes).

▶ EXCLUDED TEXTS: List all the terms that you would like to exclude from the SPL screening. There are a few terms that are common across all addresses, names, etc., and excluding them may result in fewer false hits. For example, words such as international, division, and PVT are common. Be very careful with EXCLUDED TEXTS, and test the results before moving to production. Sometimes the reduction in the number of words can trigger hits by meeting the ORIGINATING FEATURE % and actually result in increased hits.

▶ ALIAS TERMS: Use this field to screen alias names. If you have a business partner named David who also goes by Dave, then maintaining the alias as Dave allows it to be used while searching the SPL.

▶ NORMALIZATION: Normalization allows you to replace certain characters or sets of characters with different characters for search purposes. For example, you could replace "psychology" with "sychology" because they sound similar. If you maintain normalization for "psy" to "sy," the system replaces "psy" with "sy" for the SPL search any time it is used in a word. Another example might be the letter "o" with an umlaut: "ö." This is commonly spelled in English as "oe" because English does not use the umlaut. By setting up this normalization, you ensure any time the BP and SPL differ because of a translation of "ö" into "oe," the system will recognize it.

We recommend that you set up normalization after you have

tried and understood the other settings because having too many functional settings within control settings may make it difficult to interpret screening results.

▶ TREX DESTINATION: As of SAP Global Trade Services 7.2, there is an SAP TREX function with SPL screening. If you plan to use it, you need to maintain the Remote Function Call (RFC) destination for the comparison procedure. See Section 1.4 for more information on this topic.

1.7.5 Customizing/application buffer

Anytime you make a change to the SPL configuration section of GTS (SPRO/IMG), you must run RESET BUFFER to ensure that all changes in configuration are acknowledged. After resetting the buffer, follow all of the listed comparison terms processes shown discussed in Section 1.7.3.

1.8 Cross-area monitoring

1.8.1 Analyze reasons for release

This is a very useful report for auditing. You can use it not only view the results of user decisions, as in an audit trail report, but also to capture the reason for release. This report is also a good way to review the users' work and ensure they are in fact using a reason for release. The menu is shown in Figure 1.64; let's look at some of the key options on this screen.

▶ REASON FOR RELEASE: Use this option to only search releases done for a specific reason.

▶ DATE OF SPL SCREENING: This option narrows the search to the date of the SPL screening.

▶ REFERENCE NUMBER: This can refer to either a business partner number or a document number, depending on the choice you make in the REASON OBJECT field described below.

▶ REASON OBJECT: Use this field to specify either business partners or documents. Both options cannot be checked at the same time and must be audited separately.

Analyze Reasons for Release

Compliance Block				
Legal Regulation				
Reason for Release		to		⇨
Date of SPL Screening		to		⇨

Document				
Reference Number		to		⇨
Object Type		to		⇨
Logical System		to		⇨
Created by (Feeder Syst.)		to		⇨
Chgd by (Feeder System)		to		⇨
Created by		to		⇨
Created on		to		⇨

Layout	
Layout	
Reason Object	Customs Document ▾

Figure 1.64: Analyze reason for release

1.9 Compliance tips

Some common SPL misconceptions

 Sanctioned Party List checking (also known as Excluded Parties, Restricted Parties, or Denied Parties) can be a confusing process to understand. It is a common misconception that there is a "list" to check against. It is also a common misconception that a law mandates checking against a list. The truth is, there are many lists, each of which comes from a different government or non-governmental source, and each list has unique implications and intentions. Furthermore, not everyone is equally bound by all lists, nor does each apply to all transactions equally. In this section, we will review the lists, including where they come from and why we check against them. We will also discuss best practices to follow when you perform a check.

The following discussion is intended to assist you in developing your personal compliance plan. It is not possible to present a "canned" or ready-to-use plan, because every situation is different. Therefore, you must develop a customized plan for your business that takes into account all the risks you face and the unique needs and resources of your business.

1.9.1 Overview of SPL lists

In *Appendix 2*, you will find a summary of various lists that are commonly checked against. As explained in Section 1.3.1, these list names and acronyms are taken from the data provided by MK Data Services. There are other sources of SPL data that may look different, but the information contained in the lists and the general structure of the lists should be largely similar.

These lists come from various sources but generally are created by a particular country's government agency or agencies (e.g., the US Department of the Treasury). Some lists, however, come from non-government agencies such as the United Nations Security Council or the World Bank.

Similar to the variety of sources for these lists, each list also has a different application that must be understood. For example, the Treasury *OFAC* lists tend to prohibit financial dealings of any kind with a listed party. On the other hand, the Bureau of Industry and Security's Entity List does not prohibit dealings but rather requires a license, and only for those items listed. In other words, you may be able to sell a truck to a listed Entity without a license but not a fighter jet. Furthermore, the BIS "Unverified List" does not prohibit or require a license for dealings. Instead, it is intended only to serve as a "red flag." There is no requirement to stop the transaction, but you are well advised to do so and investigate further.

One thing to keep in mind is that, in most cases, there is no law requiring you to perform an SPL check at all. Rather, you are expected to comply with the rules of the list (e.g., do not deal with prohibited parties), but how you achieve compliance is your own choice. Most government agencies will not tell you how to screen the list or how to deal with "close calls." Rather, they will simply penalize you if you break the rules.

Lastly, we would like to challenge the misconception that SPL checking is purely an "export" issue. True, exporting is a high-risk activity and far more likely to result in an SPL infraction than importing or domestic transactions. However, dealing with a forbidden party in any of the three transactions noted above can result in an offense as well. In fact, most Department of the Treasury offenses relate to financial transactions and dealings, **not** the movements of goods as in an export.

United States government lists

Lists created by the United States government get the most attention on a global level. This is for several reasons:

1. They are the largest.
2. They have the most serious enforcement and penalties.
3. Many companies operate in the US.
4. They apply "*extraterritorially*" (more on that later).

Because of the above, most compilations of SPL list data are dominated by those lists published by US government agencies. Figure 1.65 shows a web page offered by the US agency "export.gov" and is intended to assist US exporters. It is important to understand, however, that some of the lists provided here apply to domestic transactions as well as exports.

This is just a sample – there are many more lists to screen against!

Note, however, that this is not an exhaustive list of US published lists. In fact, if your data is similar to the data being used by most SPL screeners, over half probably belong to the GSA Excluded Party List.

Consolidated Screening List

Below is a link to a downloadable file that consolidates export screening lists of the Departments of Commerce, State and the Treasury into one spreadsheet as an aide to industry in conducting electronic screens of potential parties to regulated transactions. In the event that a company, entity or person on the list appears to match a party potentially involved in your export transaction, additional due diligence should be conducted before proceeding. There may be a strict export prohibition, requirement for seeking a license application, evaluation of the end-use or user to ensure it does not result in an activity prohibited by any U.S. export regulations, or other restriction.

Prior to taking any further actions, users are to consult the requirements of the specific list on which the company, entity or person is identified by reviewing the webpage of the agency responsible for such list. The links below will connect you to the specific webpage where additional information about how to use each specific list is contained. These links are also embedded into the file for each listed entity to direct you to the proper website for information about how to resolve the issue. Note that the column on the attached file, which is titled "Source List", indicates which specific consolidated screening list is the source for each entry on the spreadsheet. Blank data fields in the file are not applicable to the consolidated screening list in the "Source List" column.

Department of Commerce – Bureau of Industry and Security

- Denied Persons List - Individuals and entities that have been denied export privileges. Any dealings with a party on this list that would violate the terms of its denial order are prohibited.
- Unverified List - End-users who BIS has been unable to verify in prior transactions. The presence of a party on this list in a transaction is a "Red Flag" that should be resolved before proceeding with the transaction.
- Entity List - Parties whose presence in a transaction can trigger a license requirement supplemental to those elsewhere in the Export Administration Regulations (EAR). The list specifies the license requirements and policy that apply to each listed party.

Department of State – Bureau of International Security and Non-proliferation

- Nonproliferation Sanctions - Parties that have been sanctioned under various statutes. The linked webpage is updated as appropriate, but the Federal Register is the only official and complete listing of nonproliferation sanctions determinations.

Department of State – Directorate of Defense Trade Controls

- AECA Debarred List – Entities and individuals prohibited from participating directly or indirectly in the export of defense articles, including technical data and defense services. Pursuant to the Arms Export Control Act (AECA) and the International Traffic in Arms Regulations (ITAR), the AECA Debarred List includes persons convicted in court of violating or conspiring to violate the AECA and subject to "statutory debarment" or persons established to have violated the AECA in an administrative proceeding and subject to "administrative debarment."

Department of the Treasury – Office of Foreign Assets Control

- Specially Designated Nationals List – Parties who may be prohibited from export transactions based on OFAC's regulations. The EAR require a license for exports or reexports to any party in any entry on this list that contains any of the suffixes "SDGT", "SDT", "FTO", "IRAQ2" or "NPWMD"."
- Foreign Sanctions Evaders List: Foreign individuals and entities determined to have violated, attempted to violate, conspired to violate, or caused a violation of U.S. sanctions on Syria or Iran, as well as foreign persons who have facilitated deceptive transactions for or on behalf of persons subject to U.S. Sanctions. Transactions by U.S. persons or within the United States involving Foreign Sanctions Evaders (FSEs) are prohibited.
- Sectoral Sanctions Identifications (SSI) List: Individuals operating in sectors of the Russian economy with whom U.S. persons are prohibited from transacting in, providing financing for, or dealing in debt with a maturity of longer than 90 days.
- Palestinian Legislative Council (PLC) List: Individuals of the PLC who were elected on the party slate of Hamas, or any other Foreign Terrorist Organization (FTO), Specially Designed Terrorist (SDT), or Specially Designated Global Terrorist (SDGT).

Figure 1.65: Export.Gov consolidated screening list

85

GSA Excluded Party List

The GSA Excluded Party List is a narrowly focused list of entities debarred from GSA Government Procurement. The GSA is the General Services Administration, and they are responsible for the administration of the US Federal Government's real estate and infrastructure. They also manage certain aspects of government procurement, or selling to the government.

As a result of this function, they maintain a list of *excluded parties*. These parties are debarred from selling to the government because of some past infraction. The list of debarred parties is available at *www.sam.gov*, and most SPL list subscriptions include this data.

GSA Excluded Parties are usually only relevant if (a) you are selling to the government and (b) the item you sell to the government is somehow tied to an item or service you receive from the excluded party. That said, many companies deem it prudent to simply avoid dealing with GSA-excluded parties entirely.

Extraterritorial application of US lists

Something that is unique to the United States rules is that the US will enforce the application of these rules outside of the country. For example, many of the OFAC lists are stated as applicable to all "US Persons." In the regulations, a "US Person" is defined as (among other things) any US corporation and its subsidiaries. This means that a foreign subsidiary of a US company could be held liable for a business transaction involving a Department of the Treasury forbidden party, despite the transaction occurring in another country and involving neither US citizens nor goods originating in the US

Because of this, it is well-advised that all companies screen against the US lists, regardless of whether or not they are operating in the US. There are many examples of the US applying its rules against foreign entities and individuals.

Other government lists

The US is not the only country that publishes lists of sanctioned parties. Canada, Australia, the United Kingdom, and European countries publish similar lists. While most of these lists are only binding for companies that operate or are owned in the applicable country, we recommend checking against all of these lists, for a couple reasons.

First, this will ensure you do not violate a law unknowingly. Many multinationals have very complex structures, and ownership of various divisions in different countries can often be surprisingly diverse. For example, you may be selling a good from Canada to Hong Kong, but the sales agent you employ for that region is an Australian citizen and lives there when not visiting customers in Asia. Do you know if the Australia Consolidated List may be binding on you? Better safe than sorry: it is better to review hits against foreign lists rather than to miss a violation when it is too late.

Secondly, different countries may spell foreign language names differently. For example, a name like Mohammed could be spelled as Mohamad by one country. Searching against multiple country lists will ensure the broadest range of spellings and varieties in your database, giving you greater security.

Non-governmental lists

There are also lists that are not government published, most notably, the UN Security Council and the World Bank lists. These lists are not binding in and of themselves, but often parties on these lists are added to local national lists as a result. Identifying a match before it becomes the law in your country is very wise. As a result, we encourage you to review these lists.

1.9.2 SPL List authorities and binding vs. non-binding

What follows is a non-exhaustive, quick reference guide to some common lists and advice on their binding nature and application, as well as the authority behind the list. This information should not be interpreted as legal advice; rather it is a suggested approach to SPL screening. As we indicated earlier, there is no law requiring SPL screening, only laws mandating that you do not violate the prohibition or obligations created by the list. As such, you are free to develop your own compliance method. The six examples provided below were specifically selected to show the wide variety of lists and their binding/non-binding natures. We encourage you to expand on this and do a similar review of all the lists to ensure that you have a complete understanding of the purpose and binding nature of the list in question.

GSA Excluded Parties List

Authority: General Services Administration

Binding for: Anyone selling to the US government, provided the sale to the government intersects with the activity involving the excluded party.

Application: Any purchase from the excluded party (goods or services).

Website: *www.sam.gov*

OFAC Specially Designated National Lists (e.g. SDNT, SDGT, SDNC)

Authority: Department of Treasury Office of Foreign Asset Control

Binding for: All "US Persons"

Application: These lists identify *SDN*s (Specially Designated Nationals). Depending on the specific SDN list, potentially any dealing in finance or goods and services is strictly prohibited (in other words, do not buy from them, and do not sell to them!).

Website:
http://www.treasury.gov/resource-center/sanctions/Pages/default.aspx

> ## US OFAC lists are not only for companies in the USA!
>
> Note that OFAC SDN lists tend to be extraterritorial. This means they do not only apply in the territory of the United States. Someone in a foreign country (e.g., Germany) could violate these rules if they are affiliated with a US company.
>
> Example of OFAC *extraterritorial* reach: Let us look at the Global Terrorism list (SDGT) as an example: 31 CFR 594 prohibits dealing in property or money with a listed entity. The prohibition applies to all "US Persons." Section 594.315 makes it clear that a "US Person" includes the foreign branch of any US corporation. This is generally the case will all the OFAC sanctions.

BIS Entity List

Authority: Department of Commerce, Bureau of Industry and Security

Binding for: Anyone exporting or re-exporting US origin/content goods and US persons, regardless of the origin of the good.

Application: A license may be required for the export/re-export or in country transfer of any good to an entity on this list.

Website: *http://www.bis.doc.gov/*

World Bank List

Authority: The World Bank

Binding for: Anyone participating in a World Bank-financed contract.

Application: Any purchase from a listed debarred entity.

Website: *http://www.worldbank.org/*

United Nations Security Council Sanctions (UNS)

Authority: The United Nations Security Council

Binding for: Any UN member nation that has passed as law the resolution of the council.

Application: While a UN sanction is not immediately binding on any individual nation, it is virtually assured that most members will quickly pass it as law. Once it is passed as law (ratified), then it becomes binding in that country. We recommend considering any UN sanction as valid as law, as it will likely become law very quickly.

Website: *http://www.un.org/sc/committees/*

European Sanctions List (EUS)

Authority: European Union

Binding for: Any EU member state

Application: While the EU lists are technically only binding in the EU, many non-EU countries consider this the standard to follow. As a result, the EU lists often are copied by other countries, and we recommend that you monitor them, regardless of where you operate.

Website: *http://eeas.europa.eu/cfsp/sanctions/consol-list/index_en.htm*

1.9.3 "Close matches" and what to do next

Therefore, the software implementation is done, the go-live date has come and gone, and all of the users are trained. The celebration party is already a distant memory. You are a user responsible for SPL releases and reviews. You come into work this morning and find a "match" resulting in a blocked document. You review the block for the first time since you began using the software and think you may be looking at a true match! The customer on our order may actually be the entity on the SPL list! Now what?

Unfortunately, too many users are put in this position and never properly trained on what to do with the software now that they have it. Certainly, they were trained on how to release the document. They were also shown how to place the customer on the negative list if it is a genuine match. However, they were never trained in the nuances of reviewing the SPL lists and how to deal with a "close match" or possible valid match.

Unfortunately, there is no easy answer to the question, "How do you verify a close match?" The Department of the Treasury does offer some guidance regarding how to determine matches. This information can be found on its website:

http://www.treasury.gov/resource-center/faqs/Sanctions/Pages/answer.aspx

However, you will very quickly note that this process instructs you to use it only if the "hit" is against an OFAC list. If it is another list, then it directs you to the "keeper" of that list. In practice, finding the "keeper" is not always easy. However, the guidance from OFAC is certainly good general guidance, and using these steps with any list is a good start.

Department of the Treasury guidance

 Step 1: Is the "hit" or "match" against OFAC's SDN list or targeted countries, or is it "hitting" for some other reason (e.g., "Control List" or "PEP," "CIA," "Non-Cooperative Countries and Territories," "Canadian Consolidated List (OSFI)," "World Bank Debarred Parties," or "government official of a designated country"), or can you not tell what the "hit" is?

If it's hitting against OFAC's SDN list or targeted countries, continue to Step 2 below.

If it's hitting for some other reason, you should contact the "keeper" of whichever other list the match is hitting against. For questions about:

The Denied Persons List and the Entities List, please contact the Bureau of Industry and Security at the US Department of Commerce at 202-482-4811.

The FBI's Most Wanted List or any other FBI-issued watch list, please contact the Federal Bureau of Investigation
(*http://www.fbi.gov/contact/fo/fo.htm*).

The Debarred Parties list, please contact the Office of Defense Trade Controls at the US Department of State, 202-663-2700.

The Bank Secrecy Act and the USA PATRIOT Act, please contact the Financial Crimes Enforcement Network (FinCEN), 1-800-949-2732.

If you are unsure whom to contact, you should contact your interdict software provider that told you there was a "hit."

If you cannot tell what the "hit" is, you should contact your interdict software provider that told you there was a "hit."

Step 2: Now that you have established that the hit is against OFAC's SDN list or targeted countries, you must evaluate the quality of the hit. Compare the name of your account holder with the name on the SDN list. Is the name of your account holder an individual while the name on the SDN list is a vessel, organization, or company (or vice versa)?

If yes, you do not have a valid match.*

If no, please continue to Step 3 below.

Step 3: How much of the SDN's name is matching against the name of your account holder? Is just one of two or more names matching (e.g., just the last name)?

If yes, you do not have a valid match.*

If no, please continue to Step 4 below.

Step 4: Compare the complete SDN entry with all of the information you have on the matching name of your account holder An SDN entry will often have, for example, a full name, address, nationality, pass-port, tax ID or cedula number, place of birth, date of birth, former names, and aliases. Are you missing a lot of this information for the name of your account holder?

If yes, go back, get more information, and then compare your complete information against the SDN entry.

If no, please continue to Step 5 below.

Step 5: Are there a number of similarities or exact matches?

If yes, please call the hotline at 1-800-540-6322.

If no, you do not have a valid match.*

If you have reason to believe that processing this transfer or operating this account would violate any of the regulations, you must call the hotline and explain this knowledge or belief.

The instructions above outline how to determine a hit. The next question is, who should make that determination? We will explore this question in the next section.

1.9.4 Example of a review strategy

In the following section, we will review a sample process flow for an SPL review strategy. This process represents a two-level review, with initial review by front line employees and the second by a manager or subject matter expert. The following is a quick summary of such a strategy, but keep in mind that every implementation must include a unique strategy that works best for the client. No two companies are alike in risk or structure, and no two strategies should be identical.

Note that this scenario assumes the staff authorized to release are in distribution or logistics. In your example, they can be housed anywhere, but we strongly recommended that they do **not** work in an area with a vested interest in sales or purchases. For example, if the release staff were in the sales department, their decision to release could be compromised by their desire to make the sale. The ideal candidates are in compliance or legal if possible, but realistically, many companies will choose to place the function in logistics. Logistics departments typically are viewed as more of a neutral third party to transactions and willing to delay/stop them if they violate any rules or requirements.

Also, note that this sample strategy is for business partner reviews. A separate review process for documents will also have to be crafted. The strategy is visualized in Figure 1.66.

Step 1: The initial block

SAP GTS has identified a business partner (BP) that meets the criteria set up in your configuration settings. As a result, it is blocking the BP and it will remain blocked until there is a user review and release (if appropriate).

As soon as the block has occurred, an email alert is sent to the appropriate users. Only users with authority to release the block should receive this email, but it is recommended that both levels one and two receive it. Level two reviewers (for example, a department manager) may not respond initially, but this ensures they are aware of the block if their employees are unavailable, or refer it to them as a second-level review.

Step 2: First-level review

The first-level review involves front line employees, such as a Compliance Coordinator or a Logistics/Traffic Coordinator. These employees receive the email alert as soon as there is a block and go into the SAP GTS cockpit to review the reason for the block (as per section 2(a)(v)(1) in this chapter).

The release staff makes their decision based entirely on the data found within SAP GTS. There are three logical outcomes of their review:

1. They determine a "prima facie" false hit. This means the review determines that the hit is obviously, and on face value, not a real match. For example, if the SPL entry was John Wesley Smith, and the BP was Johann Smythe Wesley, under certain configuration settings, this may trigger a hit, but it is clearly a false hit. Using the steps OFAC suggests (as shown in Section 1.9.3) is a good way to spot false hits.

2. The match is valid (or possibly valid), but the SPL entry is expired. This will only occur if you have chosen to review expired entries in your settings (See Section 1.2).

3. The match is valid (or possibly valid), so it is referred to second-level review.

If the first-level reviewer encounters either scenario one or two, they are free to release the partner, and no further review is needed. If they encounter the third scenario (valid or possibly valid match), then it must be forwarded to second-level review. Let us say in this example that the second-level review is with the manager of the Logistics Department.

It should be easy to see that variations can be needed across different companies and scenarios. For example, a very simple one—many companies may not be comfortable letting a first line reviewer release a match on account of an expired SPL entry and prefer this to be reason for a second-level review.

Step 3: Second-level review

As we saw above, the first-level review is complete and the match is deemed valid, or at least the possibility of it being valid is sufficient to force a second-level review. The second-level review likely is triggered through an email or verbal conversation between the first-level reviewer and the second. Sticking with our example, our Logistics Coordinator sends an email to the Logistics Manager requesting a further review.

The second-level reviewer will perform a more detailed review that uses data outside of SAP GTS to further clarify the situation. In this model, there are three sources of outside data:

1. SPL Website. This means actually going to the source website for the government agency responsible for the SPL list in question. Often there you will find out more regarding the entry in question or read the original executive order/federal register. Also, you can research the nature of the list and whether or not it means trade with that party is prohibited. You can read about this in Sections 1.9.1 and 1.9.2.

2. Other evidence or verification. This means plain old-fashioned investigation. Sometimes you will need to be a bit of a private investigator! If you enjoyed those old 1980s shows like Magnum PI, this will be right up your alley. Do some general internet searches to learn more about your business partner. Will verifying some key point of data be important, such as birthdate or passport number? Consider going to a third party for assistance; there are companies now that offer consulting work that can range from researching your customer all the way to visiting them in person (anywhere in the world). Ninety-nine percent of the time, Internet research will prove adequate, but be prepared for that time when your sales manager will not allow the block unless you can prove this is, in fact, the SPL-listed entity.

3. Legal advice. If concerned, go to your internal or external legal resources for advice. You may be wondering why we never mentioned the option of asking the agency in question. That's because I would leave that task to legal, as they enjoy attorney-client privilege and can make a neutral inquiry. If you are at the point where you are ready to say to an agency, "my customer may be on your list...," then leave that to the lawyers.

After all the research work, there are only two options: release the partner or leave it blocked. We recommend that, if you leave it blocked, that you place it on the negative list. This just makes for a cleaner audit trail and prevents accidental release by someone else.

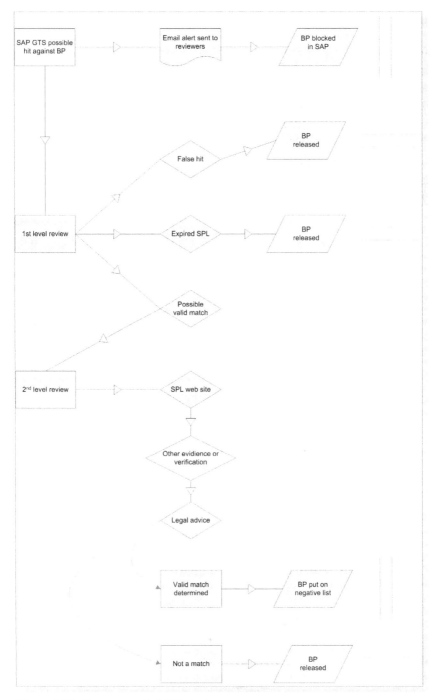

Figure 1.66: Recommended SPL review process

1.9.5   Auditing the system

You will want to implement routine audits of your SPL system. There are multiple components and aspects to the system, as discussed above, and due diligence requires you to audit its effectiveness. By "system," we do not simply mean "SAP GTS." We mean the comprehensive, total system around GTS, from configuration through subscription services to end user training. Figure 1.67 shows a high level view of the SPL "chain," if you will. A weak link or break anywhere in this system could cause a failure and non-compliance. Every one of these sections must be audited periodically.

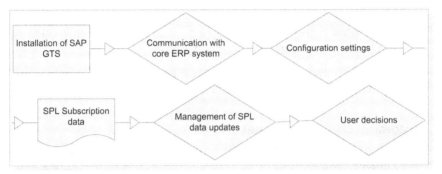

Figure 1.67: SPL chain

Suggested areas for audit:

The following section outlines some ideas for areas that you should audit. Please note that this list is not exhaustive.

GTS implementation

1. Was the implementation done properly? Are all required settings in place?
2. Did the implementation ensure all types of partners and documents would be reviewed?

Communication with ERP

1. Are all documents transferring to GTS?
2. Are all new and changed partners transferring to GTS?
3. When do they transfer?

GTS configuration

1. Do the SPL checking settings ensure that all probable matches will be caught?
2. Would a real SPL entry be caught if used in a document?
3. What if that real SPL entry was slightly misspelled?

SPL subscription data

1. Are all the legally required lists being checked?
2. Are the lists complete? (Do they match the government published lists?)
3. Are updates done immediately? (e.g., if a new SPL party listed by gov't today, when is it in subscription data?)
4. Are all SPL parties identified by their appropriate government list? (e.g., OF, AC SDN vs BIS Denied Party)

Management of SPL data updates

1. Are updates from subscription provider sent as soon as they are created?
2. Are updates loaded into GTS immediately?
3. Are updates checked against previously released parties? When?

User decisions

1. Who is releasing documents/partners?
2. What training have they received?
3. Do they have a written release process to follow?
4. Who is checking their release history?

2 Compliance

Every business transaction that crosses a border, whether outbound or inbound, needs trade compliance checks. Compliance checks involve checking all the business partners that are in the shipping document against the sanctioned party list to make sure that the country being shipped to is not under embargo, as well as checking whether the product being shipped needs a license or license exception.

Say you have an outbound delivery. Before the delivery leaves, you have to check the business partners to whom the item has been sold or shipped to, the bill-to party, the freight forwarder, and the third-party shipper. You also have to perform a sanctioned party screening against all business partners, check the countries associated with the ship-to party or the ultimate consignee where the product will land, perform an embargo check against the country where the product is being shipped, and determine the appropriate licenses against the ultimate consignee. So how does SAP GTS help?

SAP GTS can automate all of these checks to make the process faster and easier. You can configure the system to propose what licenses you will need and perform all your screening transactions and business partner checks against the denied party list. This only leaves you to look at the exceptions, such as potential matches on the denied party list. Most importantly, your trade is not bottlenecked with manually performed compliance checks that can be unpredictable and error-prone.

2.1 Import compliance checks overview

SAP GTS allows you to perform all necessary checks for both exports and imports, such as sanctioned party list screening, embargo screening, and license determination to import goods into the country. Furthermore, COMPLIANCE MANAGEMENt, a module in SAP GTS, allows you to support the monitoring of the transactions that are transferred to SAP GTS, such as embargo data maintenance, transaction review, release, and business partner review due to an embargo. All of this can be done from the LEGAL CONTROL IMPORT screen (see Figure 2.1).

To get to the LEGAL CONTROL – IMPORT screen, follow menu path SAP GTS AREA MENU • SAP COMPLIANCE MANAGEMENT • LEGAL CONTROL – IMPORT. Use the MONITORING tab to see different reports and documents such as blocked documents, payments, incomplete documents, and documents with license assignment, e.g. all the documents that were transferred to GTS. Monitoring allows you to review blocked documents (see Figure 2.2), follow the license assignment, and review assigned documents.

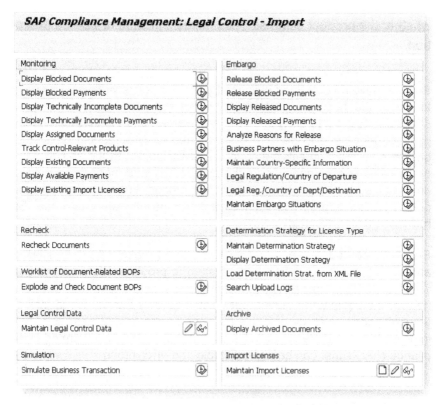

Figure 2.1: SAP Compliance Management: Legal control – import

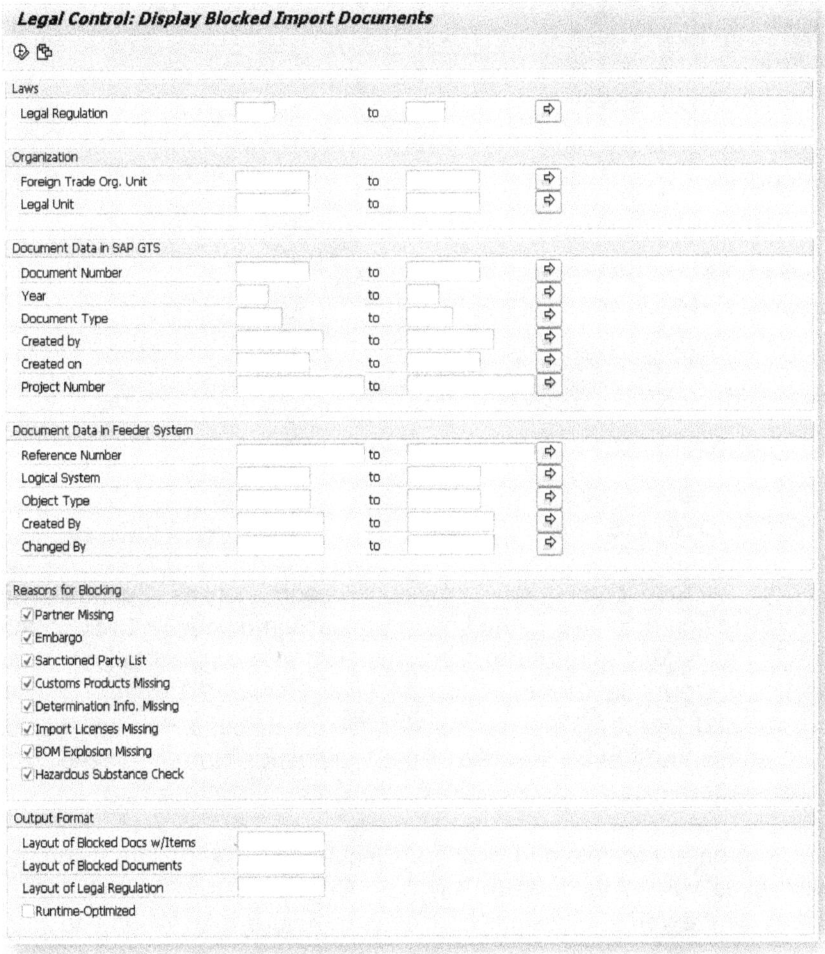

Legal Control: Display Blocked Import Documents

⊕ 🖺

Laws

Legal Regulation		to		⇨

Organization

Foreign Trade Org. Unit		to		⇨
Legal Unit		to		⇨

Document Data in SAP GTS

Document Number		to		⇨
Year		to		⇨
Document Type		to		⇨
Created by		to		⇨
Created on		to		⇨
Project Number		to		⇨

Document Data in Feeder System

Reference Number		to		⇨
Logical System		to		⇨
Object Type		to		⇨
Created By		to		⇨
Changed By		to		⇨

Reasons for Blocking

- ✓ Partner Missing
- ✓ Embargo
- ✓ Sanctioned Party List
- ✓ Customs Products Missing
- ✓ Determination Info. Missing
- ✓ Import Licenses Missing
- ✓ BOM Explosion Missing
- ✓ Hazardous Substance Check

Output Format

- Layout of Blocked Docs w/Items
- Layout of Blocked Documents
- Layout of Legal Regulation
- ☐ Runtime-Optimized

Figure 2.2: Legal Control: Display blocked import documents

The EMBARGO tab on the right side of the screen allows you to review the business partners that are under embargo and review transactions that are affected. If transactions are blocked due to an embargo, you can have the selected transaction to these countries with authorization for shipment, and then you can selectively release the transactions to processing by the supply chain. You can maintain the embargo data set up for import transactions here (see Figure 2.3).

Embargo	
Release Blocked Documents	⊕
Release Blocked Payments	⊕
Display Released Documents	⊕
Display Released Payments	⊕
Analyze Reasons for Release	⊕
Business Partners with Embargo Situation	⊕
Maintain Country-Specific Information	⊕
Legal Regulation/Country of Departure	⊕
Legal Reg./Country of Dept/Destination	⊕
Maintain Embargo Situations	⊕

Figure 2.3: Close up on Embargo options

Use the IMPORT LICENSES tab to maintain import licenses. Suppose you need to assign a license to the import transaction manually. Click on the line that says MAINTAIN IMPORT LICENSES. The system then takes you to the LEGAL CONTROL: CHANGE CONTROL DATA screen. Fill in the LOGICAL SYSTEM and OBJECT TYPE (purchase order or inbound delivery) fields. You can manually enter the data in the REFERENCE NUMBER field or use the drop-down menu.

After you enter the data and click the execute icon, the system automatically takes you to the LEGAL CONTROL: CHANGE LEGAL CONTROL DATA screen where you can assign licenses (see Figure 2.4). When you click on the execute icon, the system lists all of the items you entered in the previous screen. You can select any line and assign the appropriate classification and license. The system proposes all the available licenses. You just need to select the appropriate ones. Figure 2.5 shows the document with the assigned classification and license for the item number ten.

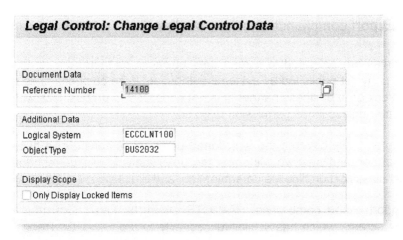

Figure 2.4: Change legal control data

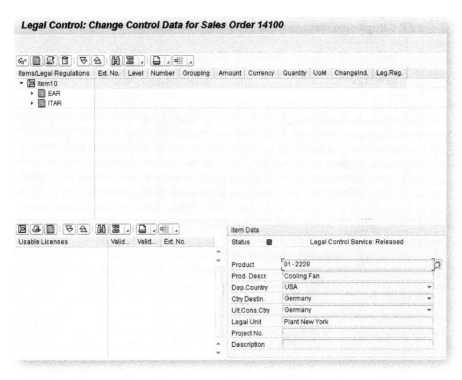

Figure 2.5: Example of legal control

2.2 Export compliance checks overview

Companies are obligated to screen their business partners against the denied party list published by customs authorities. If the company finds a hit or block on a business partner, it is not supposed to do business with the partner unless it has permission to do so.

In Chapter 1, we covered the sanctioned party list screening of a business partner, and now we will cover the other aspects of legal control: product classification, license determination, and embargo.

To support export compliance, SAP GTS offers the LEGAL CONTROL – EXPORT screen, which has similar functionality to the LEGAL CONTROL – IMPORT screen. You can get to this screen from SAP GTS AREA MENU • COMPLIANCE MANAGEMENT • LEGAL CONTROL-EXPORT (see Figure 2.6).

Figure 2.6: Legal control export menu

When you save the document in SAP ECC, the system converts the document into an export and transfers it to SAP GTS. Figure 2.7 shows the export block report that pulls the purchase order object (BUS2012), along with other outbound transactions (sales and delivery notes). Follow menu path SAP GTS AREA MENU • COMPLIANCE MANAGEMENT • LEGAL CONTROL-EXPORT • DISPLAY BLOCK REPORT.

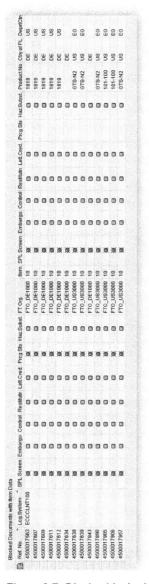

Figure 2.7: Display blocked export documents

105

With SAP GTS, you can convert Stock Transfer Orders (STO) into export orders as you transfer them from ECC to SAP GTS. Then you can perform all the necessary export checks against them.

SAP GTS compliance management also allows you to maintain the license determination within the SAP GTS cockpit as master data. Figure 2.8 shows the license types determination table. You can access this transaction using menu path SAP GTS AREA MENU • SAP COMPLIANCE MANAGEMENT • LEGAL CONTROL – EXPORT • MAINTAIN DETERMINATION STRATEGY under the section DETERMINATION STRATEGY FOR EXPORT LICENSE TYPE. This table shows the typical exporting legal regulations, destination country groups, export control classification numbers, and the possible license types. All of the license information in SAP GTS is maintained in the area menu, not in configuration. This keeps your data dynamic and focused.

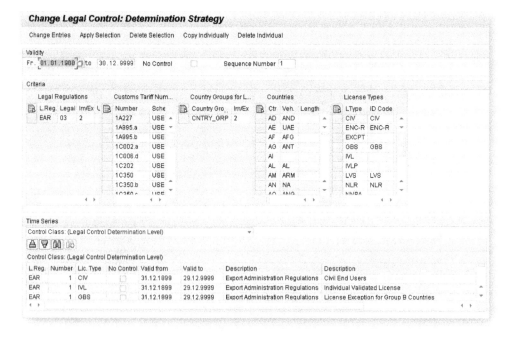

Figure 2.8: Change legal control determination strategy

The license types determination table helps you determine the license type for your export based on the exporting country's legal regulation, destination country, and product classification. See Section 2.6 for more information on license determination.

2.3 Legal control import/export

In the previous two sections, we covered import and export compliance from a business point of view, and in this section, we will cover how to address them in the system.

History of legal control in SAP GTS

 One of the key functionalities introduced with the release of SAP GTS 2.0 is legal control export/import, which has been enhanced in later releases (3.0, 7.0, 7.1, 7.2, 8.0, 10, 10.1 and the latest version 11).

Legal control export/import allows you to enable the license determination for your outbound and inbound transactions (sales and purchasing). SAP GTS enhances the license determination functionality by allowing companies to meet complex license requirements. Many business rules and settings move to the SAP GTS cockpit for easy access and ongoing maintenance.

The expanded and enhanced functionality of SAP GTS compliance allows more flexibility to handle complex business processes. You can now enable different service checks, legal controls, embargoes, and sanctioned party lists (SPLs) by document type, item category, and item category-specific settings for inclusion of service checks. You also have specific legal controls for license types and certain control settings that enable you to meet complex license requirements. For example, you can enable value and quantity depreciations from transactions and multiple licenses attributes checks, such as products, export control numbers, business partners, and foreign trade organizations.

To activate these services with specific transaction types, the path is SAP ERP REFERENCE IMG • GLOBAL TRADE SERVICES • GENERAL SETTINGS • DOCUMENT STRUCTURE • ACTIVATE DOCUMENT TYPES FOR APPLICATION AREAS.

Figure 2.9 shows the service activation for compliance with SAP GTS document types. You can selectively enable the services for document types.

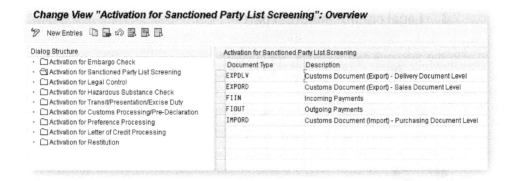

Figure 2.9: Document type activation for SPL

In Chapter 1, we covered the SPL screening functionality. Figure 2.9 shows how to activate the functionality with specific GTS document types.

Activating SAP GTS Services against SAP GTS document types does not yet tell SAP GTS what to do with incoming SAP ECC documents. To link ECC documents with SAP GTS documents, follow menu path SAP ERP REFERENCE IMG • GLOBAL TRADE SERVICES • GENERAL SETTINGS • DOCUMENT STRUCTURE • ASSIGNMENT OF DOCUMENT TYPES FROM FEEDER SYSTEMS.

Figure 2.10 shows the assignment of the SAP ECC or your feeder system document types (sales, purchasing, and delivery) to an SAP GTS document. This allows you to set specific service checks for a particular SAP ERP or logistics document.

In SAP GTS, you can define document types by the services you want to activate. For example, the service order involves service-related contract and billing, excludes no material shipment from the part number of the license determination check, and performs only SPL and embargo checks. This way you have more flexibility in terms of what services you want to invoke, selectively by order types and within the item category level. You may have licenses that are value- and quantity-dependent. SAP GTS allows you to define a depreciation group for value and quantity. When you have a license created for a specific quantity and value based on the transaction value and quantity, the license consumes and depreciates them. Figure 2.11 shows the VALUE and QUANTITY DEPRECIATION set up by ITEM CATEGORY and DEPRECIATION GROUP.

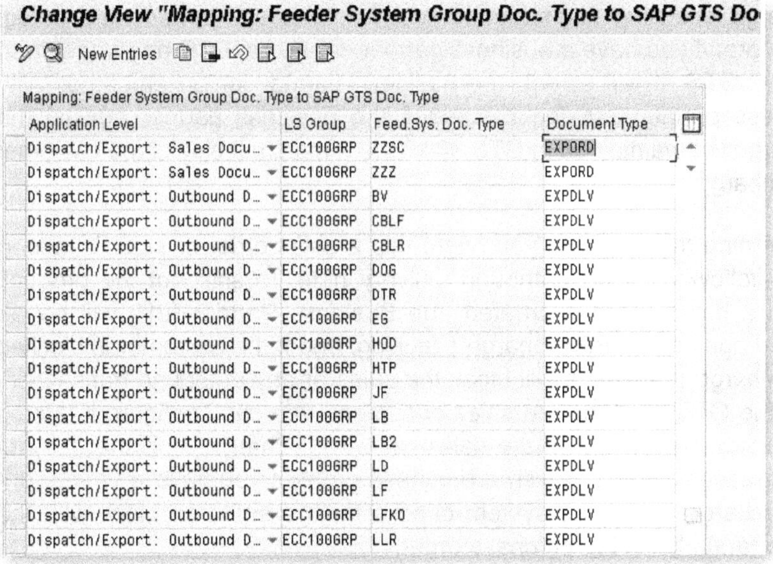

Figure 2.10: Mapping feeder system document types to SAP GTS

Figure 2.11: Item category activation

2.4   Embargo checking in SAP GTS

Today's world of trade requires your business to be able to ship and receive goods as quickly as possible. You must be ready at a moment's
notice. At the same time, governments also work just as quickly. Rela-
tionships between countries change at a moment's notice and you must
be ready for that as well. The best way to be prepared for global changes
is using embargo checking. *Embargo checking* allows you to screen the
ship-to country for export partners and ship-from country for import partners. It also allows you to block any transactions shipped to or from embargo countries.

Embargo checking is performed when a business partner is created. Therefore, if you have a business partner created in ECC and transferred to SAP GTS, it will screen the business partner for an embargo. With business partner transfer, if screens the business partner against the embargo list maintained in GTS. If it finds a match, it blocks the customer for embargo.

Concerning transactions, you might use a sales order or stock transport order, followed by an outbound delivery note, to ship out the product. When a sales order is created, the Business Partner (BP) will be reviewed against the BP embargo checking, and if the customer is blocked for embargo reasons, it will block the sales or any outbound transaction. With the GTS block on the sales document, you can configure it to stop the further processing of the sales document; that is, stop the delivery note creation. Similarly, with a purchase order, if you have a vendor under embargo block, the system checks for the embargo block with the vendor and blocks the purchase order.

SAP GTS manages embargo situations as services within compliance, and you can control the different legs for embargo or maintain different country list regulations. Most importantly, the SAP GTS master data maintains these countries, which means you do not have to go through configuration settings.

Figure 2.12: shows the embargo setting with the SAP GTS cockpit. You can access it using transaction code /SAPSLL/MENU_LEGAL • LEGAL CONTROL-EXPORT OR IMPORT • MAINTAIN COUNTRY-SPECIFIC INFORMATION. In SAP GTS, you can also maintain embargo countries for import processes or legs.

With the country-specific information, list all of the countries that you ship to or ship from, and when you double click on the entry, it will get copied over to the TIME SERIES section with default dates as shown in Figure 2.12: In the TIME SERIES section, check the EMBARGO box. However, the line that is displayed cannot be edited. To do this, you must first duplicate the line with the DUPLICATE ROW button (🗔). Next, check the box in this row and then delete the previous row.

Change Country-Specific Information

Transfer Time Series

Entries

Ctry	Country Key
IS	Iceland
IT	Italy
JM	Jamaica
JO	Jordan
JP	Japan
KE	Kenya
KG	Kyrgyzstan
KH	Cambodia
KI	Kiribati
KM	Comoros
KN	St Kitts&Nevis
KP	North Korea
KR	South Korea
KW	Kuwait

Time Series

Ctry	Embargo	Valid from	Valid to	Country Key
KP	☑	31.12.1899	29.12.9999	North Korea

Figure 2.12: Embargo settings in SAP GTS master data

Many embargos apply to both imports and exports. For embargos limited to a specific direction (inbound or outbound), you can use transaction code /SAPSLL/MENU_LEGAL • LEGAL CONTROL-EXPORT OR IMPORT • LEGAL REG. / COUNTRY OF DEPT/DESTINATION.

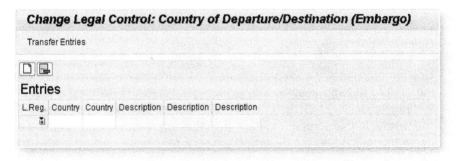

Change Legal Control: Country of Departure/Destination (Embargo)

Transfer Entries

Entries

L.Reg.	Country	Country	Description	Description	Description
🔲					

Figure 2.13: Embargo setting based on country of departure/destination

Figure 2.13 shows the master data maintenance for embargo based on the country of departure and country of destination. In the legal regulation, you need to key in the legal regulation and in the first country field the country of departure and in the second country field the country of destination. Legal regulation represents the highest entity in GTS against which the different GTS services are configured and data services are activated.

You can also have an embargo list that is specific to a legal regulation (see Figure 2.14). Legal regulations represent the country legal customs laws and regulations. Therefore, if you want to maintain an embargo list specific to a country or legal regulation for exporting from and importing into that country, you can use this functionality.

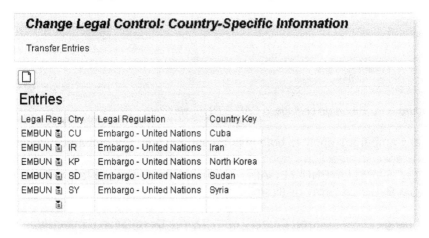

Figure 2.14: Embargo settings: legal regulation-specific

Use the functionality shown in Figure 2.14 to maintain countries that are the under embargo specific to a legal regulation. In the example shown, the regulation is EMBUN, but you can create as many regulations as necessary. In this screen, maintain the legal regulation and the country of departure or country of destination. Legal regulation can be active for export or import, and based on the activation, the country listed here will apply to those transactions (export/outbound or import/inbound).

2.5   Product classification

All goods shipped out of the US must be labeled with their five-character *Export Control Classification Number* (ECCN), license or license exception, and *Schedule B* or *Harmonized Tariff Number*. ECCN are associated with the product and describe the classification of the product in which category falls under or group and relevant control, or lack of it applies. Without a Schedule B, you cannot complete the Shipper's Export Declaration (SED), and other export declaration documentation requires these three critical pieces of trade information: ECCN, Schedule B, and License or License exception, if applied. Furthermore, you also need a Harmonized Tariff System number for import into any country around the world. You need to be able to access these numbers quickly and easily. The classification tool in the SAP GTS facilitates searching for the right number and allows you to classify and assign the classification number to a product. As product classification is a daily and ongoing activity for trade, you can pull up a work list at any given time to see products that require classification. The classification work list is one of the tools available with SAP GTS that allows you to prepare for work on a daily basis and plan your workload.

In SAP GTS, only the classification definition is done within configuration, and the actual control of data is maintained within the front end as master data. In SAP GTS, classifications are controlled by a numbering scheme, and you can even configure the structure to represent the number.

Export Control Classification Number

 An *Export Control Classification* **Number** (ECCN) is a specific alphanumeric number used to identify the level of control for an article being exported from any of the 40 countries participating in the Wassenaar Agreement. In the US, the ECCN is assigned by the Department of Commerce.

The *Harmonized Tariff System* is an internationally standardized system maintained by the World Customs Organization (WCO) for classifying traded products. Usually made up of six to ten digits, the Harmonized Tariff System classifies products for customs purposes.

2.5.1   Classification data maintenance

Classifications in SAP ECC are set at the plant level. This means that you must return to the material master for every plant when you classify a product. With SAP GTS, you can apply classifications by legal regulations. What this means is that multiple plants can share the same legal regulation if they are located in the same country. Legal regulations are defined for a country, and every regulation has an originating country. Classifications can also be set up for country groups if they are shared across multiple countries. If you have more than one country where the same regulation applies, you can activate this regulation to apply to all applicable countries. In other words, you can maintain the product classification per regulation activated only by countries where this regulation applies.

You can use the ECCN to represent the export control with the product classification and the ECCN grouping to further sub-classify and add another layer of control for the license determination or control. For example, if you have an ECCN that has a different control for retail and non-retail, you can use the ECCN group to represent retail and non-retail. Therefore, you have an ECCN that translates to the ECCN control as published by the customs authorities, and the ECCN grouping could then be used for granular control, with the same ECCN used for retail and non-retail. An ECCN group can be maintained using the menu path SAP GTS Area Menu (Transaction code /SAPSLL/MENU_LEGAL) SAP COMPLIANCE MANAGEMENT • CLASSIFICATION / MASTER DATA • EXPORT CONTROL DEFINITIONS • CHANGE CONTROL GROUPING FOR PRODUCTS, or you can use the transaction code directly /SAPSLL/CCGR).

SAP GTS also allows you to upload an XML file through the classification content, or you can maintain it manually in the system. The classification content or classification codes for import and export are identified and maintained as a numbering scheme in the SAP GTS configuration. Figure 2.15 displays the number scheme for an export control classification number, and Figure 2.16: displays the number scheme for a harmonized tariff system. The numbering scheme allows you to maintain a structure that represents the classification.

Figure 2.15: ECCN number structure

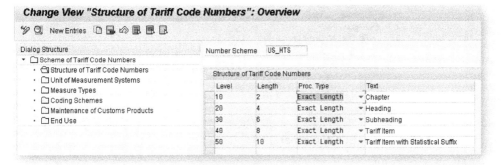

Figure 2.16: Tariff code number structure

Based on the structure maintained in the configuration, you can have the content loaded or manually maintained within SAP GTS. Use menu path COMPLIANCE (FOR EXPORT / IMPORT) • CLASSIFICATION/MASTER DATA • WITH-IN IMPORT CONTROL DEFINITION OR EXPORT CONTROL DEFINITION • MAINTAIN EXPORT OR IMPORT CONTROL CLASSIFICATION NUMBER or transaction code /SAPSLL/LLNS_002 to maintain the export number and /SAPSLL/LLNS_001 for the import number. The export commodity code and harmonized tariff number can be maintained using the menu path SAP CUSTOMS MANAGEMENT • CLASSIFICATION • (A) COMMODITY CODES • MAINTAIN COMMODITY CODES OR (B) TARIFF CODE NUMBERS • MAINTAIN TARIFF CODE NUMBERS. Alternatively, use transaction code /SAPSLL/LLNS_102 for the commodity code and transaction /SAPSLL/LLNS_101 for the HTS number. You need to enter the appro-priate numbering scheme and click on MAINTAIN NUMBERS to maintain the new ECCN manually or DISPLAY NUMBERS to display the content. Figure 2.17 displays the export control classification number content.

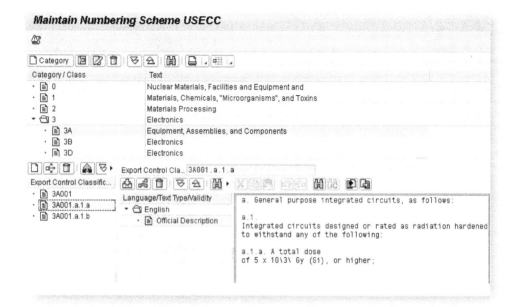

Figure 2.17: Maintain ECCN number

SAP GTS allows you to load the ECCN and the harmonized tariff system from an XML file. Content provider companies provide content in the XML format GTS accepts, and you can buy the content from them or contract with them for periodic updates. Based on the content file schedule, you can set up a process to upload these files to the GTS server. Use this function in the export or import area to load the content online from a local directory, or schedule it in background with a file located in the application server. The following transactions are delivered in GTS for content file upload:

- ▸ /SAPSLL/LLNS_UPL102 (COMMODITY CODE)
- ▸ /SAPSLL/LLNS_UPL101 (HARMONIZED TARIFF SYSTEM)
- ▸ /SAPSLL/LLNS_UPL002 (EXPORT NUMBER)
- ▸ /SAPSLL/LLNS_UPL001 (IMPORT NUMBER)

SAP GTS allows you to classify or assign an import or export classification to a product using three different methods:

1. The worklist
2. Maintain product classification
3. Reclassification

These three different classification tools facilitate product classification. The worklist provides you with a list of products that require classification.

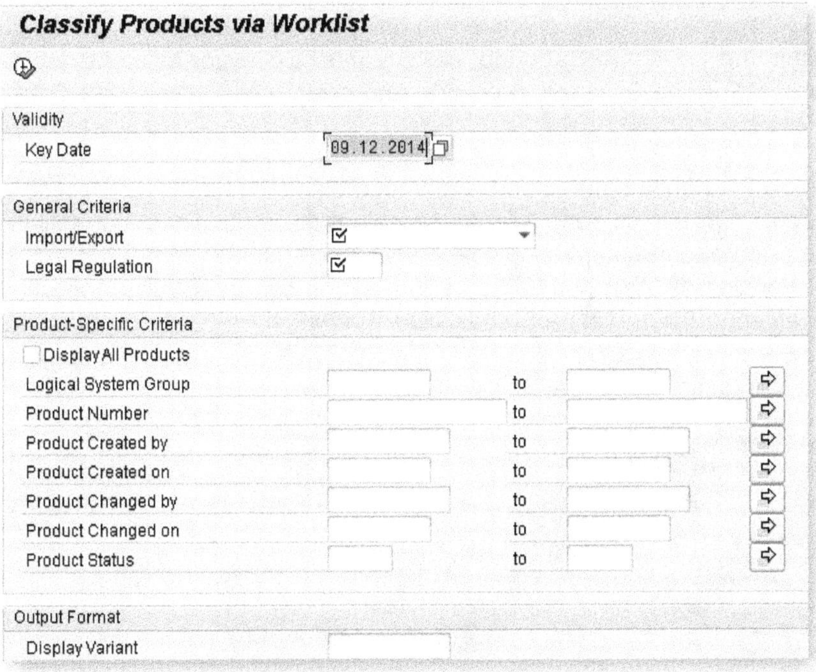

Classify Products via Worklist

Validity

Key Date	09.12.2014

General Criteria

Import/Export	☑
Legal Regulation	☑

Product-Specific Criteria

☐ Display All Products

Logical System Group		to	⇨
Product Number		to	⇨
Product Created by		to	⇨
Product Created on		to	⇨
Product Changed by		to	⇨
Product Changed on		to	⇨
Product Status		to	⇨

Output Format

Display Variant	

Figure 2.18: Classify products via a worklist

The worklist is a classification tool as shown in the selection screen in Figure 2.18. You can filter based on the data selection available. Based on the data selection, users can work on the worklist and search products based on description. The worklist also provides functionality to mass assign the classification to products. In other words, if you have multiple products falling under the same classification, you can use the mass assignment functionality to assign the same classification to all of the products, instead of assigning one at a time. SAP GTS provides a worklist for export, import, commodity code, and HTS number individually within the respective area menu. For export and import numbers, use the menu path SAP COMPLIANCE MANAGEMENT • CLASSIFICATION / MASTER DATA • IMPORT OR EXPORT VIEW FOR CUSTOMS PRODUCTS • CLASSIFY VIA WORKLISTS AND FOR COMMODITY CODE AND HTS NUMBER, SAP CUSTOMS MANAGEMENT • CLASSIFICATION • CLASSIFICATION WITH COMMODITY CODE OR TARIFF CODE NUMBERS • CLASSIFY PRODUCTS VIA WORKLIST.

The worklist provides features to search for classifications based on specific search criteria and allows you to keep it in the clipboard for future reference. Maintain product classification functionality allows you to classify both the ECCN and the harmonized tariff system in one view. Figure 2.19 displays the function where you have different tabs for classification. Within the LEGAL CONTROL tab, classify the ECCNs for different regulations and in the CLASSIFICATION tab, and assign the HARMONIZED TARIFF SYSTEM.

Figure 2.19 shows the export and import classification assignment to a product. On this screen, you can see all of the regulations that actively are listed and the numbering scheme for the regulation where the export control classification number is assigned. You can go to this transaction by entering the transaction code /SAPSLL/MENU_LEGAL to get to the GTS AREA MENU • CLASSIFICATION / MASTER DATA • MAINTAIN PRODUCT, or use transaction code /SAPSLL/PRODUCT_02.

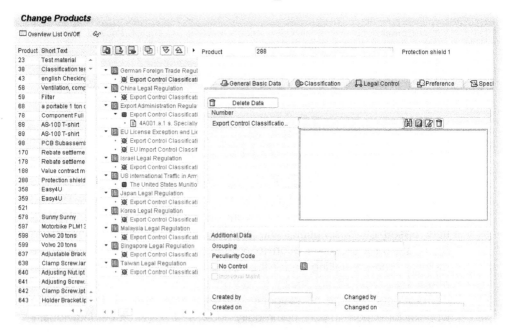

Figure 2.19: Classify product screen

Reclassification allows you to change or assign a new classification number to the product. In other words, if you have a product classified, you can use the reclassification to change it to a new number. Customs authorities periodically publish changes to the classification, which might affect your product classification, and you can use this function to apply the changed classification to the product. When you click on the reclassification transaction, the report will propose the old classification number and a new classification number. When you execute, it replaces the existing number with the new number you entered. Similar to other features for export, import, commodity code, and harmonized tariff number, SAP GTS provides functionality to reclassify the respective numbers under SAP COMPLIANCE MANAGEMENT • CLASSIFICATION / MASTER DATA FOR EXPORT AND IMPORT NUMBER AND SAP CUSTOMS MANAGEMENT • CLASSIFICATION FOR COMMODITY CODE AND HARMONIZED TARIFF SYSTEM FOR RECLASSIFICATION manually, or XML upload file.

2.6   License determination

License determination is among of the most important functionality in any global trade compliance solution. In any business transaction, be it purchase orders or sales orders, you are dealing with business partners (vendors, customers) and a product or service. The product or materials being shipped are given a number and description that is understood by your customer and vendor. For exports or imports, products are classified further so that the customs authorities understand them in the exporting and importing country.

Usually the exporting country imposes control over products based on the classifications. For example, certain products based on the classification might not be allowed to export to a certain country or customer due to its application and risk. Some products may be allowed, but only with the permission of the controlling agency in the form of a license.

Some products might generally be subject to a license requirement but be eligible for certain license exceptions. This means that they generally require an export license, but in certain circumstances, do not.

As you can see, the license landscape is complex, requiring understanding of classifications, license requirements, and exception possibilities.

Change View "Legal Control: License Type": Details

New Entries

Dialog Structure
- Legal Control: License T
  - Allowed Status

Legal Reg.   EAR   Export Administration Regulations

Legal Control: License Type

License Type	ENC-R	Encryption - Restricted

Number Range Interval   01
Import/Export   Export/Dispatch
☐ Enh. Authorization Check

Determination

☑ Multiple Licenses   ☐ Harmonized Depreciation
Objects to Be Checked

☐ Foreign Trade Org.	☐ Product No.	☑ Doc. Number
☐ Legal Unit	☑ Control Class	☐ Check First Doc. In Document Flow
☑ Business Partner	☐ Peculiarity Code	☐ Country of Dest./Depart.
☐ PartnerFunction	☐ Import Code No.	Part. Grp. Ctries
Partner Grp Functions	☑ Country Group	☐ Mult. Part. Countries
Partner Group Check	☐ Project	☐ Bus.Trans.Ty

Update

☐ Value Update	Basis for Value Upd.
Value Assignment Level	Specification of Maximum Value for All products
Value Change	No Change of Maximum Value Possible
Exceeded (in %)	Overrun Percentage Based on Total Value

Figure 2.20: Define license type

SAP GTS has enhanced this license type by adding more attributes and features (status, control settings, partner type checking, and customer-defined procedures for license type determination). More attributes allow you to define licenses with stricter control and accuracy. For example, before a license can be assigned, all of these attributes need to be satisfied. Use the ALLOWED STATUS functionality to maintain the status for a license, such as active or expired. Figure 2.20 displays the definitions available in the license types in SAP GTS.

Change View "Legal Control: License Type": Details

🖉 New Entries 🗅 🕞 🕼 🗟 🗟 🗟

Dialog Structure

- ▼ 🖾 Legal Control: License T
  - • 🗀 Allowed Status

Legal Control: License Type

License Type	IVL	Individual Validated License

Number Range Interval	81
Import/Export	Export/Dispatch
☐ Enh. Authorization Check	

Determination

☐ Multiple Licenses   ☐ Harmonized Depreciation

Objects to Be Checked

☐ Foreign Trade Org.	☑ Product No.	☐ Doc. Number
☐ Legal Unit	☑ Control Class	☐ Check First Doc. In Document Flow
☑ Business Partner	☐ Peculiarity Code	☐ Country of Dest./Depart.
☐ PartnerFunction	☐ Import Code No.	Part. Grp. Ctries
Partner Grp Functions	☑ Country Group	☐ Mult. Part. Countries
Partner Group Check	☐ Project	☐ Bus.Trans.Ty

Update

☐ Value Update	Basis for Value Upd.	Value of Goods
Value Assignment Level	Specification of Maximum Value for All products	
Value Change	No Change of Maximum Value Possible	
Exceeded (in %)	Overrun Percentage Based on Total Value	
Shortfall (in %)	No Percentage Shortfall	
☐ Low-Value Check	Aggregation Rule	
Exchange Rate Type		

Figure 2.21: Configure license type

As you can see in Figure 2.21, there is functionality to check multiple agreements, which allows you to check multiple licenses to fulfill a quantity or a license requirement. For example, if your particular license does not meet the quantity requirement, the system can look for another license value to meet the remaining quantity. You can also define the percent overflow for tolerance. For every attribute selected, you can select how many values you want maintained in the system.

SAP GRC

 SAP Governance, Risk, and Compliance GTS is a standalone product that can interface with SAP and non-SAP systems for export and import compliance, customs, and trade preference services. It enables companies to automate their trade processes embedded within the supply chain with appropriate country regulation checks, access to relevant partners, and communication to customs authorities.

121

Export or import regulations require a determination process to see if a license is required. The license determinations consider the product classification, and based on the classification, determine if a license is necessary. The results can be:

- ► License required
- ► No license required
- ► License required but exception available

Classifications are assigned to products and based on the country of departure or destination; the system picks up the relevant legal regulation and uses the license determination table to determine the license types. License types are codes that represent licenses, exceptions, or no license required in the system.

SAP GTS moves trade data to business user access within the master data, one of the frequently maintained and updated information. In addition, SAP GTS provides programs to upload the content through XML interfaces. With SAP GTS, you maintain trade data manually with tools available to maintain them. Use the transaction code /SAPSLL/MENU _LEGAL>CLASSIFICATION/MASTER DATA to maintain the classifications. Trade data and products need to be assigned with these classifications to enable the export and import compliance check and report them in the trade declarations and documents.

Many companies take the approach of mapping ECCN to ECCN grouping one-to-one in order to enable the LEGAL CONTROL • LICENSE DETERMINATION function.

In SAP GTS, the ECCN group can be an additional attribute to the product classification, and you can use it for additional control. For example, if you want to have a different control for retail and non-retail, you could define an ECCN grouping to control the license determination. As this is the core of legal control, and they represent the export control for product shipment, the SAP GTS cockpit maintains these with the trade user access.

COUNTRY GROUP consists of multiple countries and NUMBER represents the export control classification number. In this determination, the license types are determined by the active legal regulation, by the departure country for export, and by the destination country for import. The country group is picked based on the partner country in the document and classification assigned to the product.

Another important functionality is the content maintenance for harmonized tariff number and commodity codes (see Figure 2.22). In SAP GTS, you have options to upload the content using an XML interface. You have to load this content initially and continually, as the regulation updates the changes to the HTS and commodity codes. SAP GTS also provides functionality to review the product that is impacted due to the new codes and provides functionality to replace the old code with new ones. In SAP SD FT, the configuration maintains them, while SAP GTS maintains them under cockpit for trade user access. SAP GTS also provides XML upload programs.

Configuration maintains and moves the codes across systems using transports.

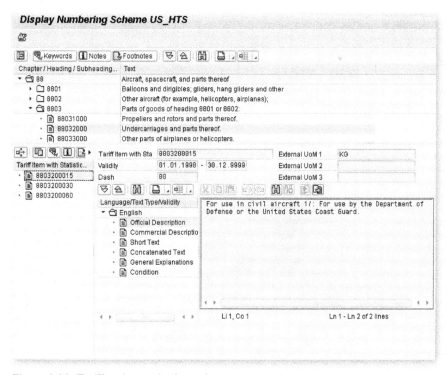

Figure 2.22: Tariff code numbering scheme

Compliance checks are performed for export and import throughout the order cycle: sales order, fulfillment, and invoicing. Another key functionality with license is that you can determine license based on partner type. You can have multiple search strategies for license type determination. You can configure it to set up text determinations based on the license type (e.g., if the business has a requirement to print a particular text for a particular license type). In specific cases, for example, a special comprehensive license, you might have a requirement to print special instructions on a trade document. While maintaining a license, the system allows you to maintain text, and you can choose to print that in the trade documents. You can set up the license type to track both quantity and value depreciation. The compliance functionality extends to import as well. The import checks can be performed throughout the purchasing cycle, purchase order, and inbound goods movements.

As of SAP GTS 7.2, functionality to support the ITAR regulation (International Traffic Arms Regulations) with the legal control called agreements was introduced, and it has been further enhanced with new releases (see Figure 2.23). Agreements are like a license within a license, or in other words, a *nested license*.

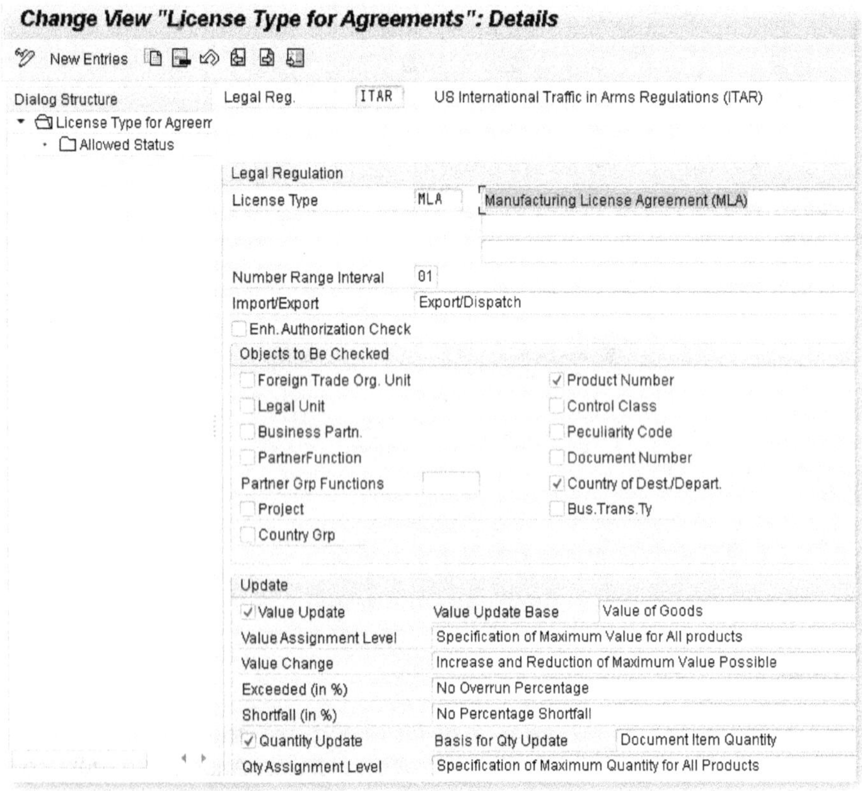

Figure 2.23: Define agreement For ITAR

Typically, a defense shipment might involve multiple licenses and the approval of one might depend on the overall agreement. Therefore, when the agreements are defined, they refer to the license type. When document is checked, it checks against the agreement, and the agreement, in turn, has the licenses associated with it.

As of SAP GTS 8.0, you can run license determination against the final product as well as the components in it if you have a bill of product or material associated with it (see Figure 2.24). At the Department of Defense, the authorities would like to run a license determination against the entire component that constitutes a product and not just the final product. Even with civil regulations, if the product components can be applicable as dual use, the license determination might be applied to components.

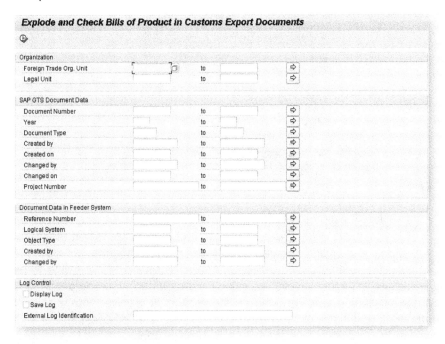

Figure 2.24: Explode and check BOP

Within the Legal Control Service, you need to enable the BOP check to determine all BOP items. Figure 2.25 displays the configuration step.

125

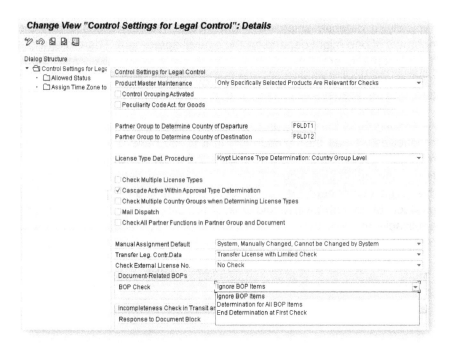

Figure 2.25: Control settings for legal service

The menu path for this configuration can be found using the following menu path: SAP GTS REFERENCE IMG • SAP GLOBAL TRADE SERVICES • SAP COMPLIANCE MANAGEMENT • "LEGAL CONTROL" SERVICE • CONTROL SETTINGS FOR "LEGAL CONTROL" SERVICE.

Another key functionality release with GTS 8.0 is the re-export check on relevant products. When you export product, it is not only important that you check the export regulation of the exporting country but also the country it is been shipped to. Furthermore, if this product is going to be re-shipped from the country receiving it (re-exported), the end destination of the product is also important. If the product is received into a country and the intent is to ship it to a different country after processing, then the re-export law of the originating country can still apply.

2.6.1 Export compliance check on outbound sales transactions based on routes

Following a compliance check and clearance, the system grants permission to create a declaration document, which is generated from the billing document. The recommended document type is the proforma billing type

126

because the export compliance check might not just be checking against the departure country and the destination country. The shipment might pass through a third country before it finally reaches its destination. For example, a shipment sent to Germany might first land in Belgium, move to France, and finally reach Germany. As of SAP GTS 7.2, you can perform export compliance checks based on the route the shipment takes. If the route includes an embargoed country, you might have to use a different route for the shipment. In some cases, it may be allowed with the appropriate license.

You can achieve legal control (license determination) by setting up route determination and turning on the indicator for it in SAP ERP REFERENCE IMG • SALES AND DISTRIBUTION • SAP GLOBAL TRADE SERVICES – PLUG IN • CONFIGURE CONTROL SETTINGS FOR DOCUMENT TRANSFER. Select the APPLICATION LEVEL (SD0A) and click DOCUMENT TYPES. Within the document type transfer configuration, select LEGAL CONTROL – DETERMINE TRANSITED COUNTRIES under DETAIL CONTROL (see Figure 2.26).

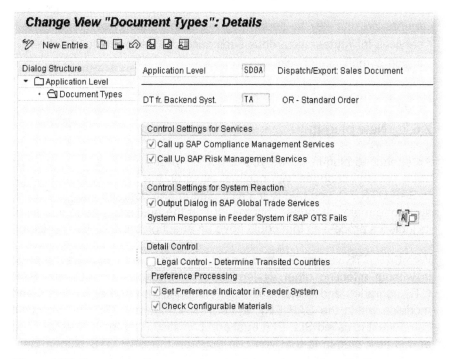

Figure 2.26: Export compliance service check based on route activation

Choose desired check type

 In Figure 2.26, the document type CALL UP SAP COMPLI-ANCE MANAGEMENT SERVICES is selected. This enables a compliance check on the logistics transaction, or document type (OR – Standard Order). If you select the check box under DETAIL CONTROL, the system performs a route check.

What are documents?

 Within the SAP system, key functions and activities are registered as *documents*. This could be a sales order for acknowledging the sales contract between a company and the customer or a purchase order contract for goods or services between a company and the vendor. **Documents** are the key to performing the compliance check from trade services for routes, hazardous substance checks, or inbound delivery import compliance checks.

2.6.2 New plug-in

An enhanced plug-in allows you to update your system for regulatory or trade process changes with minimal effect on the logistics system. Prior to SAP GTS 7.2, you had to install a plug-in and upgrade your SAP ERP system to make changes. This meant that the business had to test all of its logistics processes that could have an effect on the SAP ERP system.

With SAP GTS version 7.2 and higher, you are able to upgrade the plug-in without affecting other system plug-ins. You can manage any SAP GTS upgrades and implementations independent of other functions and modules within the SAP ERP system (see Figure 2.27). The technical component is called SLL-PI (Legal and Logistics Plug-In). The advantage of this new plug-in is that you can upgrade the SAP GTS plug-in independent of the central plug-in and without having to upgrade the SAP ERP system.

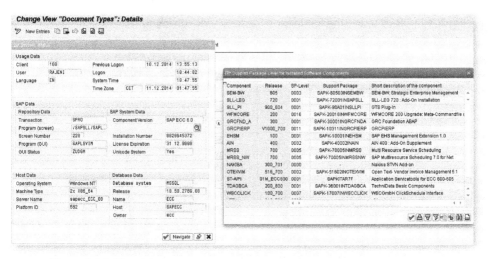

Figure 2.27: Plug-in's:

2.6.3 Shipment consolidation

Typically, goods leaving for the same geographic locations are consolidated into one commercial document or customs declaration document. This helps companies save costs because they do not have to manage or track them separately. Proforma documents, created against the delivery document, trigger customs documents in SAP GTS for generating the trade declaration documents.

In SAP ERP, a shipment document is used for consolidating deliveries. In the past with a consolidated shipment, you needed to manage the tracking of the consolidation, or have the freight forwarder manage the customs declaration on your behalf. With proforma consolidation prior to the SAP GTS 7.2, customers used the billing due list (transaction VF04).

Billing due list referred the deliveries for consolidation. Once the shipment was created, the delivery documents had to be manually entered to the billing due list to generate the consolidated proforma. With the functionality in SAP GTS 7.2 and higher, you can simply enter the shipment number. This shipment number has all of the deliveries associated with it, helping you avoid any duplicate manual effort and error.

Figure 2.28 shows the selection screen for creating a consolidated proforma based on the billing document, outbound delivery, shipment number, or load. In this example, the shipment consolidation transaction pulls the deliveries associated with the shipment and generates the consolidated proforma.

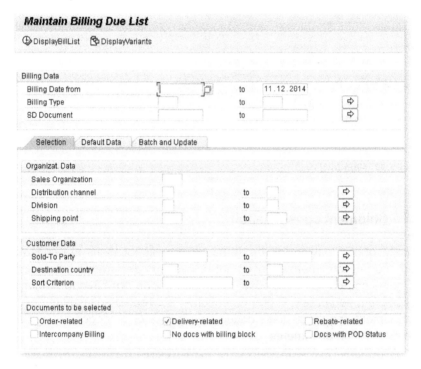

Figure 2.28: Proforma consolidation

2.6.4 Dangerous goods

If your company deals with hazardous substances or dangerous goods, you have to capture that information and manage it in your logistics process while maintaining trade and declaration compliance. You must screen your transactions for any hazardous substances. Like outbound deliveries, the inbound deliveries are required to go through compliance checks, denied party list changes, or license requirements.

As part of the compliance check, you are required to manage the logistics of the hazardous substances, as well as track and perform compliance checks. If the document is blocked due to an environmental, health, and safety check, the document can be released following the review. For example, some countries have a ban on bringing the hazardous material into the country or require hazardous material be packed and reported separately.

You can also identify dangerous goods within the customs declarations documents. Figure 2.29 shows the DANGEROUS GOODS indicator and DANGEROUS GOODS NO. field under the SPECIAL INFORMATION section. For more information on hazardous goods functionality in SAP GTS, see Section 2.8.

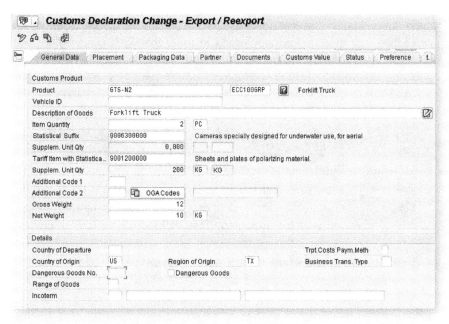

Figure 2.29: Customs declaration change

2.7   ITAR

Imagine a defense equipment manufacturing company wants to bid on the design of an equipment or control system that can be used in a missile or fighter jet. Before it can even engage on the bid and share specific product information, the US State Department requires the exporter to apply for a technical assistance agreement (TAA) to facilitate the sharing of information. The TAA operates similarly to a license, and you can designate it for a specific product, USML, customer, country, and so on.

When an exporter wants to ship physical goods out of the country, the company needs to apply for an export license, such as a DSP-5 (Permanent Export). The application for this license must reference the existing and valid TAA associated with the project involved with this sale or shipment. The application of the DSP-5 must take into account the attribute on the TAA such as dates, values, quantities, and so on. Temporary export for public exhibition, trade show, air show, or related event, even if the physical goods were licensed previously for public exhibition, require a DSP-73 (temporary export).

For situations such as these, you can use the agreements and license type functionality features in SAP GTS Compliance Legal Control. We will show you the configuration steps to meet the ITAR requirement with license types referencing agreements and how they are managed in the system. We will look at the example at a defense manufacturing company and see how the agreements are used for initial export shipments and then referred within the license type for subsequent shipments.

ITAR

 The US International Traffic in Arms Regulations (ITAR) stipulates that US importers and exporters must follow certain standards to operate with defense-related material and technologies. This includes the requirement to obtain different licenses based on the US Munition List (USML). The **three main categories of licenses** include hardware licenses, technical assistance agreements (TAA), and manufacture license agreements (MLA). Some cases call for multiple licenses across different processes.

2.7.1 Configuration steps

Let's review the configuration steps for ITAR.

Step 1: Define agreements. As of GRC GTS 7.1, SAP introduced compliance legal control agreements functionality. As explained in the scenarios above, the company will have to start the information sharing in terms of design document as a technical agreement. As a first step, we need to configure agreements. Follow menu path SPRO • SAP GLOBAL TRADE SERVICE • COMPLIANCE MANAGEMENT • LEGAL CONTROL • DEFINE TYPES OF AGREEMENTS (see Figure 2.30). After you create an agreement, the system references it by the license type. While defining the agreement in the OBJECTS TO BE CHECKED section, you need to select attributes within the transaction that you need to validate before assigning the agreement to the document or transaction. Check the value and quantity, and update the value and gross weight respectively. Also, make sure that you define a depreciation group to use in the agreement quantity and value update. To do so, follow menu path SPRO • SAP GLOBAL TRADE SERVICE • COMPLIANCE MANAGEMENT • LEGAL CONTROL • DEFINE DEPRECIATION GROUP IN AGREEMENTS. Once there, create a name and description for the depreciation group. The depreciation group helps to accumulate the value and quantity depreciation. Once defined, it needs to be assigned in the agreement definition.

Agreements vs. licenses in SAP GTS

 Agreements are a specific requirement for ITAR controls. You will not need this functionality to manage licenses for some other controls such as the Export Administration Regulations (EAR). An ITAR Technical Assistance Agreement (TAA) is the overarching agreement between your organization and the Department of State Defense Trade Controls (DTC). This agreement will control everything from what you are manufacturing to your sharing of product details with foreign nationals. It will also govern your permission to export. Note that you will still generally need to get a transactional license for each shipment. Think of the TAA as blanket permission (it may state that you can sell 100 units of a controlled product per year). Each transactional license will also have a quantity limit, and the sum total of each license must not exceed your TAA. GTS will link the licenses to the TAA and monitor this for you.

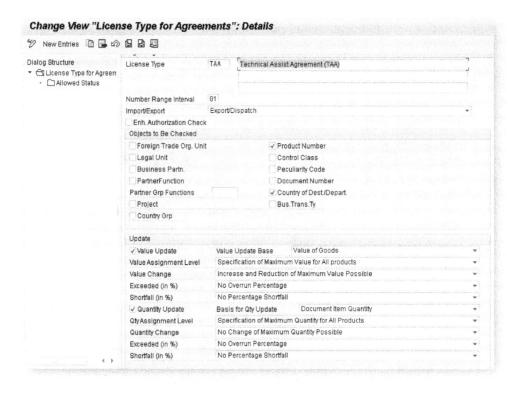

Figure 2.30: License type for agreements

Step 2: Define license type and assign agreement. ITAR uses temporary and permanent licenses and as explained, we might have to refer these licenses to the previous agreement. *License type* defines the attributes that you would like to have in the license. To define the license type, you need to select the object to be checked, value, and quantity to update. Follow menu path SPRO • SAP GLOBAL TRADE SERVICE • COMPLIANCE MANAGEMENT • LEGAL CONTROL • DEFINE LICENSE TYPES to display the license type definition. The definitions of attributes appear when you create licenses. When you scroll down in the license type definition, you need to assign the agreement type to the license types. Figure 2.31 and Figure 2.32 display the agreement assignment to license types.

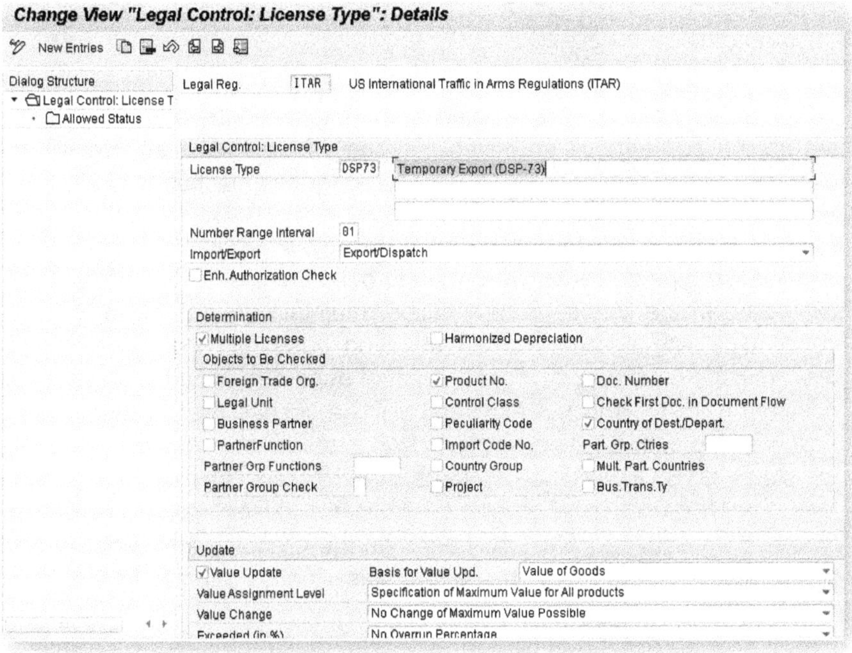

Change View "Legal Control: License Type": Details

🎲 New Entries 🗋 🖫 🖉 🖫 🖫 🖫

Dialog Structure	
▼ 🗐 Legal Control: License T	Legal Reg. ITAR US International Traffic in Arms Regulations (ITAR)
· 🗀 Allowed Status	

Legal Control: License Type

License Type DSP73 [Temporary Export (DSP-73)]

Number Range Interval 81
Import/Export Export/Dispatch ▼
☐ Enh. Authorization Check

Determination
☑ Multiple Licenses   ☐ Harmonized Depreciation
Objects to Be Checked

☐ Foreign Trade Org.	☑ Product No.	☐ Doc. Number
☐ Legal Unit	☐ Control Class	☐ Check First Doc. in Document Flow
☐ Business Partner	☐ Peculiarity Code	☑ Country of Dest./Depart.
☐ Partner Function	☐ Import Code No.	Part. Grp. Ctries
Partner Grp Functions	Country Group	Mult. Part. Countries
Partner Group Check	☐ Project	☐ Bus.Trans.Ty

Update
☑ Value Update   Basis for Value Upd. Value of Goods ▼
Value Assignment Level   Specification of Maximum Value for All products ▼
Value Change   No Change of Maximum Value Possible ▼
Exceeded (in %)   No Overrun Percentage

Figure 2.31: License type definitions with attributes

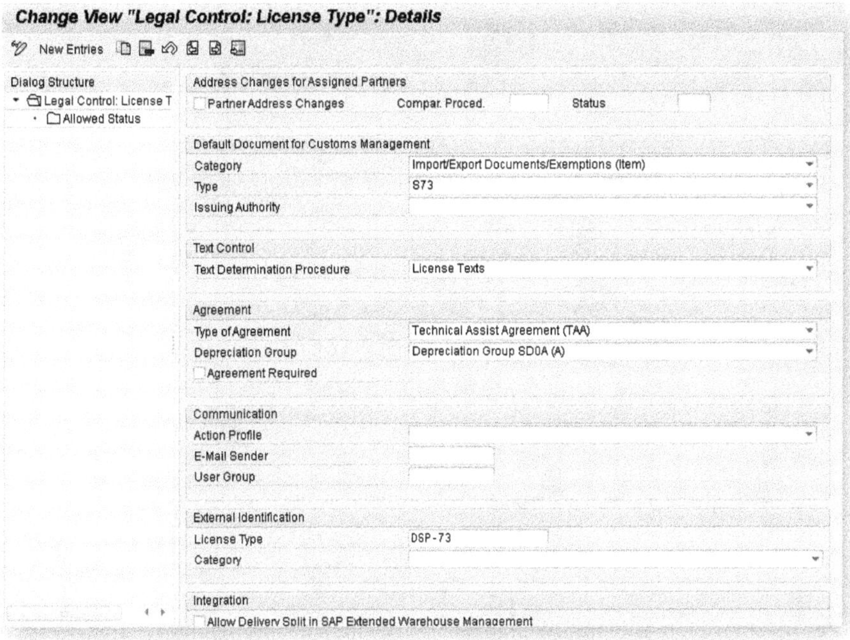

Change View "Legal Control: License Type": Details

🎲 New Entries 🗋 🖫 🖉 🖫 🖫 🖫

Dialog Structure	
▼ 🗐 Legal Control: License T	Address Changes for Assigned Partners
· 🗀 Allowed Status	☐ Partner Address Changes Compar. Proced. Status

Default Document for Customs Management
Category Import/Export Documents/Exemptions (Item) ▼
Type S73 ▼
Issuing Authority ▼

Text Control
Text Determination Procedure License Texts ▼

Agreement
Type of Agreement Technical Assist Agreement (TAA) ▼
Depreciation Group Depreciation Group SD0A (A) ▼
☐ Agreement Required

Communication
Action Profile ▼
E-Mail Sender
User Group

External Identification
License Type DSP-73
Category ▼

Integration
☐ Allow Delivery Split in SAP Extended Warehouse Management

Figure 2.32: Assignment of agreement and depreciation group to license type

In the AGREEMENT tab, make sure you assign the TYPE OF AGREEMENT and DEPRECIATION GROUP you created in Step 1.

GTS data set ups: The steps noted above explained the configurations to set up the agreements and license types. In the next step, we will go over the master data set up that is required for this function to work.

Step 3: Build your determination strategy. Following the agreement and license type definition, you need to build the license type determination table. In the license determination, maintain the search logic for license type and agreement determination based on the determination procedure. For example, based on the departure country, destination country, trouping, and USML (Number), the license type is determined. Follow menu path GTS COCKPIT (TRANSACTION CODE — /SAPSLL/MENU_ LEGAL) • GTS COMPLIANCE MANAGEMENT • LEGAL CONTROL – EXPORT • MAINTAIN DETERMINATION STRATEGY. Build the table against the license type and agreement (**AGREM**) based on the grouping for hardware and technical agreement for the respective classification number.

Figure 2.33 shows the table that displays the legal regulation, grouping, departure country, classification number, and license type based on the license type determination procedure you defined.

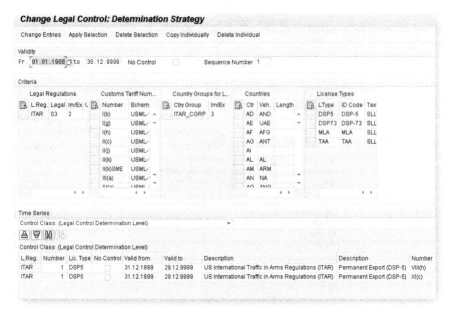

Figure 2.33: License type determination strategies by grouping for license type and agreement

Under CRITERIA, select LEGAL REGULATION, GROUPING, COUNTRIES (DESTI-
NATION FOR EXPORT), NUMBER (USML), and the relevant license type.
Click on COPY INDIVIDUALLY and you will see the entries appear under
TIME SERIES.

Step 4: Create agreements. Follow menu path GTS COCKPIT • COMPLI-
ANCE MANAGEMENT • LEGAL CONTROL – EXPORT • MAINTAIN AGREEMENTS
(see Figure 2.34). Based on the agreement defined in the configuration
in Step 1, you can maintain the agreements here.

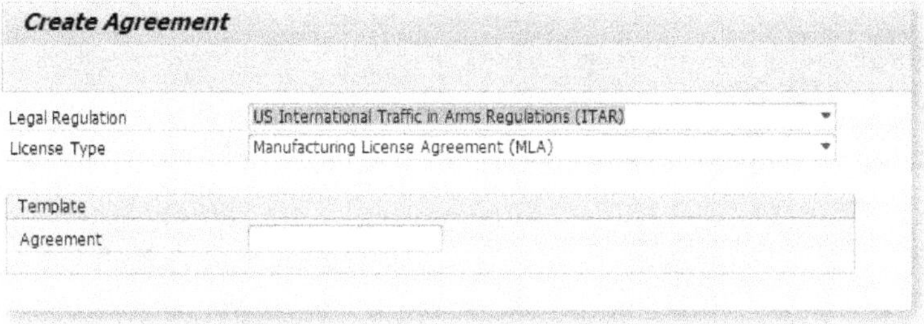

Figure 2.34: Create agreement based on the legal regulation and license type

When you click on CREATE AGREEMENT, it will bring up the screen shown
Figure 2.34. Figure 2.35 shows the details behind the agreement when it
is created. As you can see, based on the attributes selected in Step 1,
they appear when you create the agreement, value, quantity, control
classes, and country of departure/destination.

*Figure 2.35: Agreement created with status active and other attributes as defined
in configuration*

137

Step 5: Create licenses. Once you have an agreement in place, you can create licenses. When you create the license with the agreement assigned in the configuration, it is required to reference the agreement. A license can be created using the menu path GTS COCKPIT • GTS COMPLIANCE MANAGEMENT • LEGAL CONTROL – EXPORT • MAINTAIN EXPORT LICENSES • CLICK ON CREATE. When you create a license for the license type defined in Step 2 of the configuration, the system asks for an agreement reference (see Figure 2.36). You will have to enter the legal regulation and license type and select the agreement type and agreement number that you want to assign to this license from the drop-down menu.

Figure 2.36: Create license with agreement reference

You can use an agreement created in Step 4 in the agreement reference to create a license. After you enter the details in the field shown in Figure 2.36 and click CONTINUE, it will bring up the screen shown in the Figure 2.37. You need to fill in the EXTERNAL LICENSE NUMBER based on the license approval received and the VALID FROM and VALID TO. The value and quantity are derived from the agreement and should not exceed the agreement quantity and values. Within the control, you maintain the USML number and Country of Dept/Destination, and destination country. The status maintains the audit of the license when it was created, when it was applied for, and active or expired information.

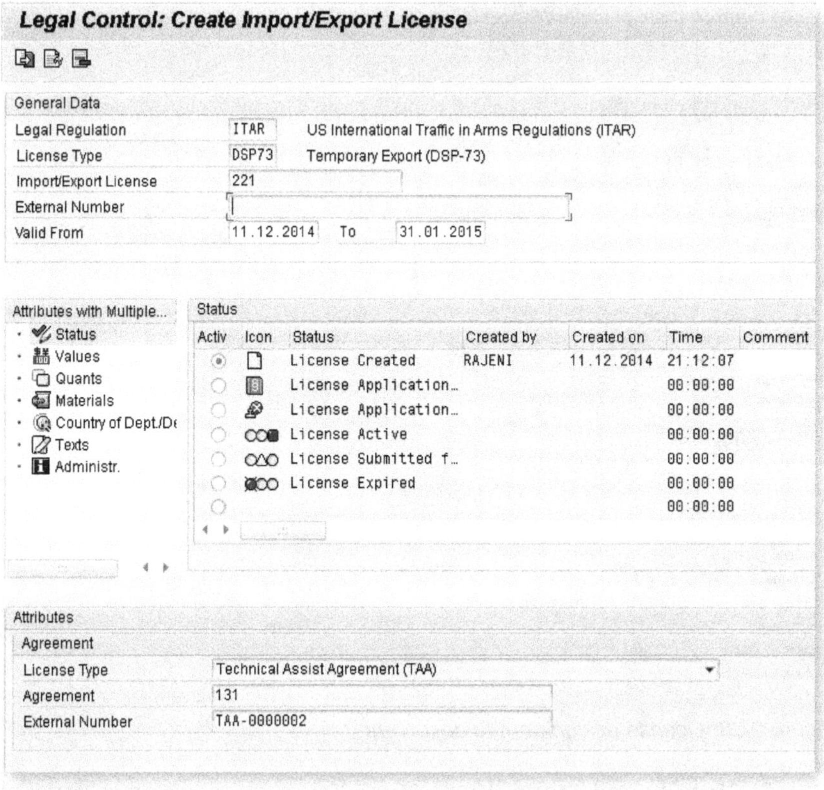

Legal Control: Create Import/Export License

General Data

Legal Regulation	ITAR	US International Traffic in Arms Regulations (ITAR)
License Type	DSP73	Temporary Export (DSP-73)
Import/Export License	221	
External Number		
Valid From	11.12.2014 To	31.01.2015

Attributes with Multiple...

- Status
- Values
- Quants
- Materials
- Country of Dept./D(
- Texts
- Administr.

Status

Activ	Icon	Status	Created by	Created on	Time	Comment
●		License Created	RAJENI	11.12.2014	21:12:07	
○		License Application…			00:00:00	
○		License Application…			00:00:00	
○		License Active			00:00:00	
○		License Submitted f…			00:00:00	
○		License Expired			00:00:00	
○					00:00:00	

Attributes

Agreement

License Type	Technical Assist Agreement (TAA)
Agreement	131
External Number	TAA-0000002

Figure 2.37: License display with agreement referenced

You can create agreement with reference to another license type or agreement. When you display the agreement, you can see the license type that is assigned to the agreement. In the center, with the details of LType (License Type), License Number, Ext. No., Valid from, and Valid to. Figure 2.38 displays the license type assigned to the agreement. This can accessed using the menu path GTS COCKPIT • GTS COMPLIANCE MANAGEMENT • LEGAL CONTROL – EXPORT • MAINTAIN AGREEMENTS • CLICK ON DISPLAY.

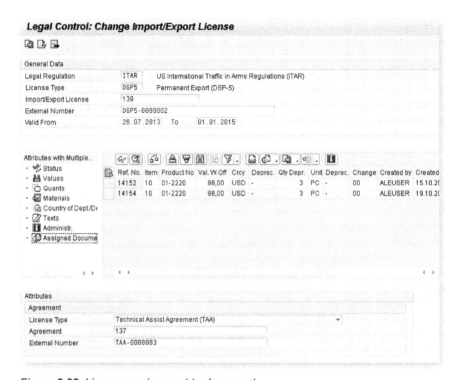

Figure 2.38: License assignment to document

Step 6: Classify and group the product. You need to assign material or products with the classification number (USML). These classification numbers and grouping in turn determine the license and agreement based on the license determination strategy you maintained in Step 3. Follow the menu path GTS COCKPIT • GTS COMPLIANCE MANAGEMENT • CLASSIFICATION/MASTER DATA • UNDER EXPORT VIEW FOR CUSTOMS PRODUCTS • MAINTAIN PRODUCTS and click on CHANGE. While you are here, you need to assign the USML classification in the export classification number and grouping (see Figure 2.39). You can search for the number and group from the drop-down list.

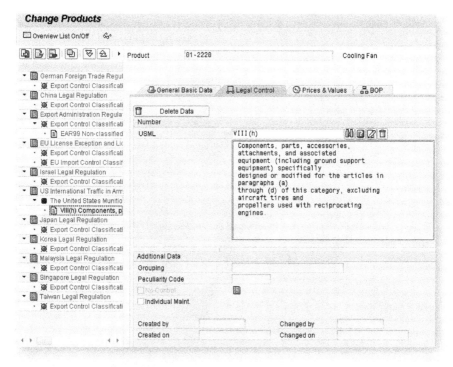

Figure 2.39: Change products (ITAR)

Step 7: Assign transaction of the agreement and license. Based on the configuration setting and GTS cockpit setting, when you create the sales order, you assign a license type and agreement. Figure 2.40 displays the log in SAP GTS following the sales order being saved in ECC. The document assignment to the agreement and license can be found using the menu path GTS COCKPIT • GTS COMPLIANCE MANAGEMENT • LEGAL CONTROL – EXPORT • DISPLAY ASSIGNED DOCUMENTS. You can use the sales order number in the REFERENCE NUMBER field and click on execute. In the report, if you click on the log, it will bring up the screen shown in Figure 2.40

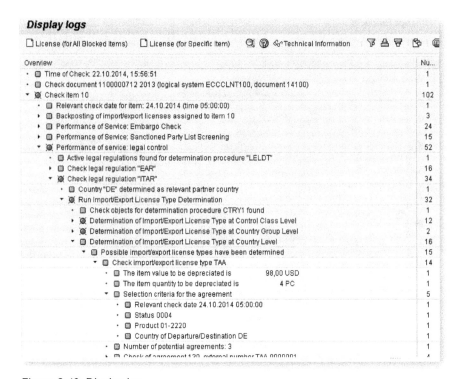

Figure 2.40: Display log

The first line item displays the license type assignment based on the legal regulation, destination country from the document, and the classification and grouping assigned to the product in **Step 7**.

Now that we have seen the document with the agreement and license type assigned, let's go back to the agreement and license type display and view the updates there.

When you display the license (see Figure 2.41), you can see the value and the quantity written off as seen in the display log in Figure 2.40. Use the menu path

GTS COCKPIT • GTS COMPLIANCE MANAGEMENT • LEGAL CONTROL – EXPORT • MAINTAIN AGREEMENTS • CLICK ON DISPLAY.

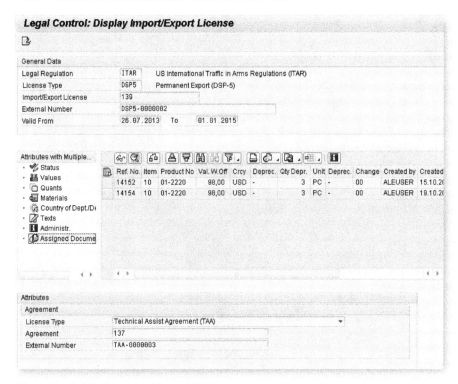

Figure 2.41: Display import/export license

Let's look at the updates to the license. The menu path is GTS COCKPIT • GTS COMPLIANCE MANAGEMENT • LEGAL CONTROL – EXPORT • MAINTAIN EXPORT LICENSE • click on DISPLAY (see Figure 2.42 and Figure 2.43).

Figure 2.42: Display license (value allocated)

To summarize, we created an agreement and assigned licenses to the agreement. We then classified the product. When the product was used in a sales order, based on the departure and destination country, it picked up the appropriate license and agreement. We might have gotten an agreement for a technical agreement, and when the actual product was shipped, we were able to refer to that. The display log showed the agreement, the license assignment, and the value and quantity depreciated. Once we saw the transaction assignment, we also confirmed the update to the license and agreement. Agreement values are decremented based on the licenses assigned, and license value and quantity are decremented based on the transaction.

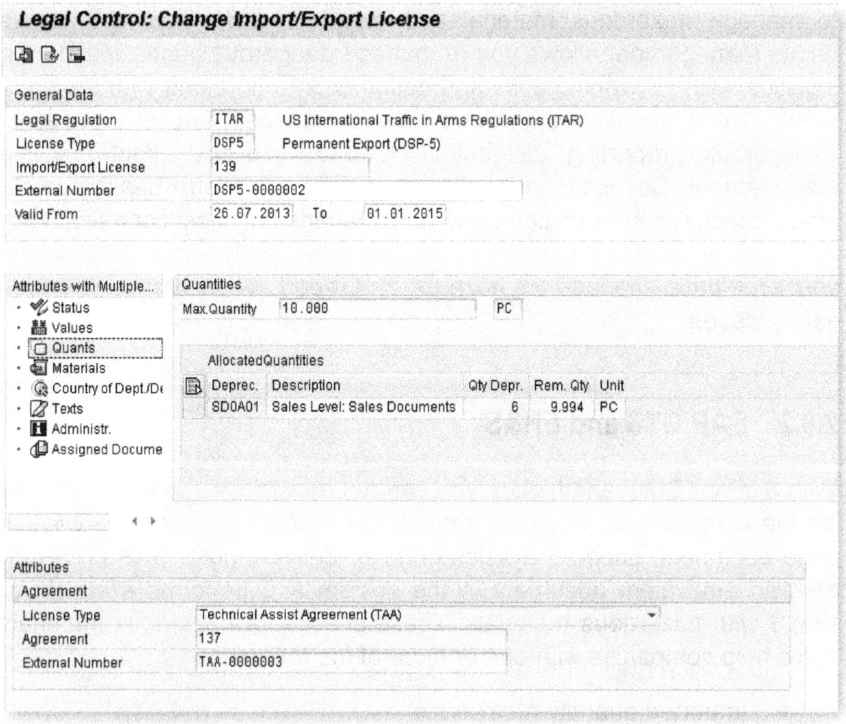

Legal Control: Change Import/Export License

[icons]

General Data

Legal Regulation	ITAR	US International Traffic in Arms Regulations (ITAR)
License Type	DSP5	Permanent Export (DSP-5)
Import/Export License	139	
External Number	DSP5-0000002	
Valid From	26.07.2013 To 01.01.2015	

Attributes with Multiple...
- Status
- Values
- Quants
- Materials
- Country of Dept./De
- Texts
- Administr.
- Assigned Docume

Quantities

Max.Quantity 10.000   PC

AllocatedQuantities

	Deprec.	Description	Qty Depr.	Rem. Qty	Unit
	SD0A01	Sales Level: Sales Documents	6	9.994	PC

Attributes

Agreement

License Type	Technical Assist Agreement (TAA)
Agreement	137
External Number	TAA-0000003

Figure 2.43: Display license (quantity allocated)

2.8   EH&S

Environment, Health, and Safety (EH&S) are guidelines or federal regulations in different areas, including environmental, occupational health
and safety, community health and safety, and construction and decom-
missioning. EH&S in SAP ECC comprises of several components, such
as basic data and tools, product safety, hazardous substance, dangerous
goods management, waste management, occupational health, and industrial hygiene and safety.

2.8.1   ECC EH&S functionality

Basic data and tools allow you to manage the specifications for all other
components, like hazardous materials and dangerous goods, centrally.
Product safety allows you manage hazardous substances with material
safety sheets, labels, etc. Hazardous substance management allows you

to manage hazardous material and report to authorities. Dangerous goods management allows you to manage dangerous goods within your logistics, with relevant checks and documents to go along with the shipment. Waste management allows you to manage disposal processes, transportation reporting, distribution of waste, and cost effect of waste management. Occupational health allows you to perform health surveillance checks with your company and manage the questionnaire. With industrial hygiene and safety, you can organize safety and hygiene within your enterprise, manage the hazards, and report events that could cause safety issues.

2.8.2   SAP GTS and EH&S

With SAP GTS 7.2 and higher, you can run hazardous substance checks for the items in your logistics transactions. When you create a compliance document, such as a sales order or delivery note, SAP GTS creates an equivalent document in the system and performs a check for EH&S with hazardous materials. These checks for hazardous materials could help companies with one or more of the following:

► Imported quantity restrictions
► Import restrictions for product from specific country of origin
► Export restrictions to specific countries
► Export quantities restrictions

Based on the hazardous substance in the logistics document, when transferred to SAP GTS, the system performs a compliance check and updates the status in the GTS customs document. Within the logistics document processing, you can check for this status, and if it is not okay or blocked, you can stop the next process step. For example, if you have a sales order line blocked due to a hazardous material, you can use the set up in the system to stop the delivery note creation. If there are restrictions on the quantity, the system can check for the quantity that is allowed.

This same check also can be applied to inbound goods for importing goods into the country through purchase orders and goods receipts logistics transactions. The function module that is in SAP ECC for performing an EH&S check on purchase order is shown in Figure 2.44 and Figure 2.45.

146

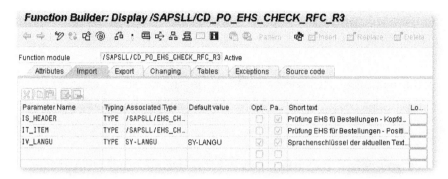

Figure 2.44: Function module /SAPSLL/CD_PO_EHS_CHECK_RFC_R3 to check EHS with PO

The input parameters have a header, item, and language key, and the export or the output from this function module returns block or okay.

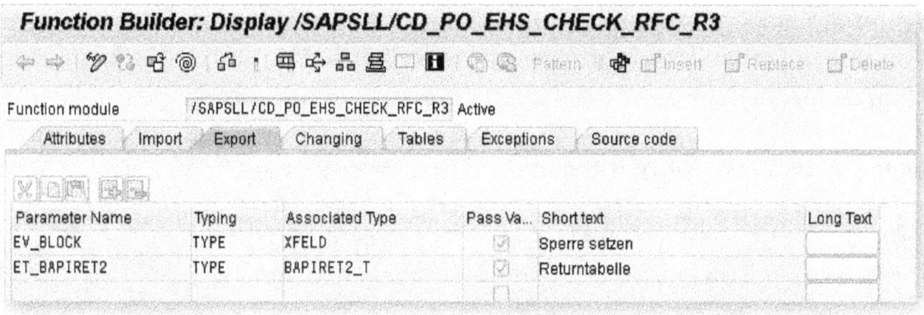

Figure 2.45: Return value and barrier set as export or output of the function module

The function module shown in Figure 2.45 is invoked for a purchase order EH&S call to GTS and check. Let us walk you through the configuration steps that are required for a hazardous material/substance compliance check. There are two parts to the setup: the first set of steps is in the SAP ECC system, and the second set is in the SAP GTS system.

2.8.3   ECC IMG activities

In the SAP ECC system, you need to set up the configuration for hazardous substance information capture and tracking with the logistics documents. We will go over the required steps to enable that in SAP ECC.

Step 1: Define the specific scenario. This might apply to the specified scenarios or category of scenario. Specify the setting for these scenarios or scenario categories, such as the quantities that can be determined from purchasing, sales, or production data.

The menu path for the configuration can be reached using the following menu path: SAP REFERENCE IMG • ENVIRONMENT, HEALTH AND SAFETY • PRODUCT SAFETY • SUBSTANCE VOLUME TRACKING • SPECIFIC SCENARIOS • click on SPECIFIC DATA DETERMINATION PER REGULATION AND SCENARIO (see Figure 2.46).

Here you define the system data determination for individual scenarios and regulations and the next step in the process. If a function module is entered separately for substance determination for the material and for the component explosion in an entry without a specified scenario, the components are filled independently of the scenario. Otherwise, they are filled according to the scenario.

When defining scenarios, you can delete scenarios that are not required. You are not permitted to define new scenarios. You are not permitted to change the assignments of scenarios and scenario categories delivered with the system. If you specify your own function modules, their interfaces must match those of the standard function modules.

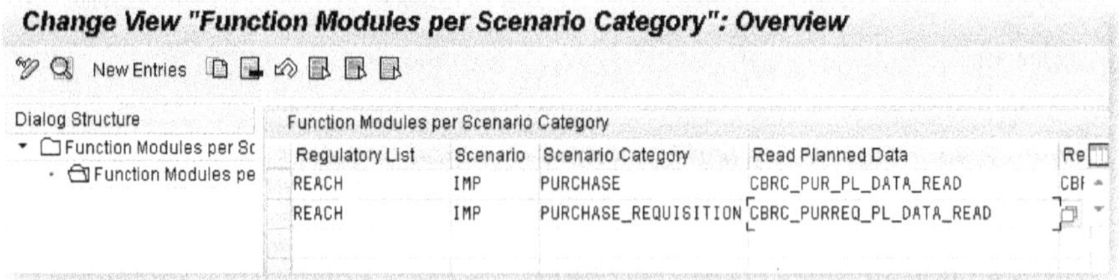

Figure 2.46: Function modules per scenario category

Step 2: Specify the selection criteria for volume tracking.

Here you specify the selection criteria for the data from system tables (e.g., purchasing, sales, delivery). You can thus restrict the logistics data that is monitored and specify, for example, which documents are tracked in substance volume tracking. If you want to restrict substance volume tracking and monitoring to specific transactions, you can use the respective table with the field TCODE. If you want to restrict substance volume tracking and monitoring in the online checks to specific transactions, you can use the table SYST with the field TCODE.

Configuration menu path is SAP REFERENCE IMG • ENVIRONMENT, HEALTH AND SAFETY • PRODUCT SAFETY • SUBSTANCE VOLUME TRACKING • SPECIFIC SELECTION CRITERIA FOR VOLUME TRACKING.

In substance volume tracking, the system reads logistics data from the following tables depending on the scenario. The different tables are maintained by updated scenario, scenario type tables, or date for planned quantities. The date for planned quantities determines the monitoring period and the year to which the quantity is assigned. To process confirmed quantities, the posting date in the material document (MKPF-BUDAT) is decisive for all scenarios. For scenario PRO (production), only the entries in table MSEG (material documents), where the order number (AUFNR) is not equal to zero, are relevant to substance volume tracking. The number of material documents to be evaluated can be reduced by filtering the relevant valuation types (field BWART).

Use table MARA to define selection criteria for the materials being monitored. In addition, you can classify materials as relevant to substance volume tracking in the classification view of the material master. This classification is read if you enter the standard function module CBRC_ MM_REL_MATNR_FILTER under SPECIFY SCENARIOS in the DETERMINE MATERIAL configuration. The options described above for selectively restricting the materials for substance volume tracking affects the transfer of data from the property tree (report RREGCH_FILL). In addition, in the standard system the data transfer program reads selection settings for table ESTRH (specification headers) from the property tree to filter out specifications that are not relevant for material assignment. Use these filter options to limit the volume of data that is transferred from the property tree to the tables for substance volume tracking.

It is better to specify material-related selection criteria independently of scenario. You need to specify scenario-specific criteria if the function modules for substance determination per material and component explosion are defined per scenario in the IMG activity SPECIFY SCENARIOS. Figure 2.47 details the mapping of the regulation, scenario, table field, sequence, and inclusion or exclusion.

Change View "Specify Selection Criteria for Volume Tracking": Overview

New Entries

Specify Selection Criteria for Volume Tracking

Regula...	Scenario	Table	Field	Se...	Include/Exclude	Sel.
REACH		MARA	MTART	0	Include	Not
REACH	IMP	EBAN	BSTYP	1	Include	Equ
REACH	IMP	EKKO	BSART	0	Exclude	Equ
REACH	IMP	EKKO	BSART	1	Exclude	Equ
REACH	IMP	EKKO	BSTYP	0	Include	Equ
REACH	IMP	EKKO	BSTYP	1	Include	Equ
REACH	IMP	EKPO	PSTYP	0	Include	Equ
REACH	IMP	EKPO	PSTYP	1	Include	Equ
REACH	IMP	MARA	KZUMW	0	Include	Equ
REACH	IMP	MARA	MTART	1	Include	Equ
REACH	IMP	MKPF	VGART	0	Include	Equ
REACH	IMP	MSEG	EBELN	0	Include	Not
REACH	PRO	AUFK	AUTYP	1	Include	Equ
REACH	PRO	AUFK	AUTYP	2	Include	Equ
REACH	PRO	MKPF	VGART	0	Include	Equ
REACH	PRO	MSEG	AUFNR	0	Include	Not
REACH	PRO	MSEG	BWART	0	Include	Bet
REACH	PRO	PLAF	OBART	1	Include	Equ
REACH	PRO	PLAF	REMFL	1	Include	Equ
REACH	PRO	RESB	BDMNG	1	Include	Not
REACH	PRO	RESB	MATNR	1	Include	Not

Position...   Entry 1 of 21

Figure 2.47: Specification of selection criteria for volume tracking

Step 3: Specify quantity limits and reactions on overall status (see Figure 2.48).

Here you specify the quantity limits that apply in the individual regulations for substances that must be tracked. For each regulation, you can specify several quantity thresholds. For the quantity thresholds, you can specify the limit values. The general quantity limit value contains the quantity limit values from the regulation, for example: Quantity threshold 1: up to 1 tonne Quantity threshold 2: 1 to 10 tonnes Quantity threshold 3: 10 to 100 tonnes Quantity threshold 4: above 100 tonnes.

When you specify the general quantity limit values, the limit values must be specified so that every possible quantity of a substance can be assigned to a quantity threshold. The upper limit value for the highest quantity threshold must contain the maximum value possible. If you specify a time period, the limit values apply for this time period. If you do not specify a time period, the limit values apply for a calendar year. The relative quantity limit value specifies the percentage value of the general quantity

150

limit value that must be exceeded before the system carries out an action.

Change View "General Quantity Limit Values": Overview

✎ New Entries ☐ ☐ ✍ ☐ ☐ ☐

Dialog Structure	General Quantity Limit Values						
▼ ☐ General Quantity Limit V:	Regulatory List	Threshold	Lower Quanti...	Upper Quanti...	U...	Period	
• ☐ Relative Quantity Lim	NOTICHCK	1				TO	
	REACH	1		1,0000		TO	
	REACH	2	1,0000	10,0000		TO	
	REACH	3	10,0000	100,0000		TO	
	REACH	4	100,0000	1.000,0000		TO	
	REACH	5	1.000,0000	999.999,9999		TO	

Figure 2.48: General quantity limit values

The menu path for the configuration can be found under SAP REFERENCE IMG • ENVIRONMENT, HEALTH AND SAFETY • PRODUCT SAFETY • SUBSTANCE VOLUME TRACKING • SPECIFIC QUANTITY LIMITS AND REACTIONS ON OVERALL STATUS.

A general quantity limit value (e.g., tonnes) must always exist for a relative quantity limit value to which the relative limit value refers. There must always be at least one relative quantity limit value for each quantity threshold (see Figure 2.49). Otherwise, an error message appears in the application log. By specifying different relative limit values for a quantity threshold, you can determine that the system carries out actions in stages, for example, that the system informs you when 70 percent is exceeded and blocks the business process when 100 percent is reached.

Change View "Relative Quantity Limit Values": Overview

✎ New Entries ☐ ☐ ✍ ☐ ☐ ☐

Dialog Structure		
▼ ☐ General Quantity Limit V:	Regulatory List	REACH
• ☐ Relative Quantity Lim	Quantity Threshold	4

Relative Quantity Limit Values				
Message Type	Rel.LimVal	Disp.Mess.	Send Mess.	Proc.Block
Information	▾ 70	☑	☐	☐
Warning	▾ 90	☑	☑	☐
Error	▾ 100	☑	☑	☑

Figure 2.49: Relative quantity limit values

If the property tree does not contain a specific quantity limit value for a substance, the quantity limit of one applies. You can specify the quantity that was registered for the substance (registered quantity) in the sub-

151

stance property tree. This quantity is the quantity limit for the substance and overrides the general quantity limit in this configuration setting. You can also specify relative quantity limits for a substance, which override the relative quantity limits. If you do not specify relative quantity limits for a substance, the system uses the relative quantity limits from this configuration setting whose general quantity limit contains the registered quantity of the substance.

For example, you have specified a registered quantity of 25 tonnes in the substance, but you have not defined relative quantity limits. In this configuration setting, you have defined the following quantity limits: Quantity threshold 1: up to 1 tonne. Quantity threshold 2: between 1 and 10 tonnes. Quantity threshold 3: between 10 and 100 tonnes. Quantity threshold 4: above 100 tonnes. Then, the system uses the relative quantity limits for the substance that you entered in this configuration setting for quantity threshold 3 and relates the percentage values to 25 tonnes. When evaluating the quantity thresholds, the lower limit of an interval is not part of the interval, but the upper limit is. This means that a quantity of, for example 10 tonnes, is assigned to quantity threshold 2, not quantity threshold 1.

Step 4: Set up online checks (see Figure 2.50).

In the online checks in substance volume tracking, the system checks whether quantity limits are exceeded during certain actions in different locations. Thus, a quantity limit can be exceeded if, for example, you create a purchase order, manufacturing order, or sales document for a material for which a substance is assigned that is relevant for volume tracking. To perform this function, follow the menu path:

SAP REFERENCE IMG • ENVIRONMENT, HEALTH AND SAFETY • PRODUCT SAFETY • SUBSTANCE VOLUME TRACKING • SET UP ONLINE CHECKS • click SET UP ONLINE CHECKS.

To set up these online checks, follow these steps:

1. Specify how the system collects the orders and documents that are relevant for the online checks.
2. Specify how the system determines the substance quantities that are relevant for the online checks.
3. Specify how the system determines whether a quantity limit is exceeded.

4. Specify how the system blocks the follow-on documents (the next document creation in the process, e.g., do you want the delivery to be blocked if the sales order has an issue) and collects and outputs messages when a quantity limit is exceeded.

If you specify a regulation in an entry, the entry applies for this regulation only. If you do not specify a regulation in an entry, the entry applies for all regulations. If the system finds two entries, for example, one with the relevant regulation specified and one without a regulation, the system applies the more specific entry. So that the system runs the online checks at various points, you must set up the checks in customizing in the appropriate customer exits and Business Add-Ins (BAdIs).

Change View "Define Function Modules for Online Checks": Overview

✏ 🔍 New Entries 🗋 🖬 🗞 🖪 🖫 🖫

Define Function Modules for Online Checks

Regulatory List	Scenario	Scenario Category	Relevance Check	Vol
NOTICHCK	EXP	DELIVERY	CBRC_LIPS_CHCK_RELEVANT	
REACH	EXP	DELIVERY	CBRC_LIPS_CHCK_RELEVANT	CBI
REACH	EXP	SALES	CBRC_SO_CHCK_RELEVANT	CBI
REACH	IMP	PURCHASE	CBRC_PUR_CHCK_RELEVANT	CBI
REACH	IMP	PURCHASE_REQUISITION	CBRC_PURREQ_CHCK_RELEVANT	CBI
REACH	PRO	PRODUCTION	CBRC_PRO_CHCK_RELEVANT	CBI

Figure 2.50: Define function modules for online checks

Step 5: Specify data transfer (property tree).

In this step, specify how the system determines the substance data that it requires for substance volume monitoring and tracking from the property trees for the substances to be tracked and writes the data to the tables in substance volume tracking (see Figure 2.51). You also specify how the system transfers the condensed quantity of a substance to be tracked to the property tree for the substance. This transfer serves to archive the total substance quantity determined over a monitoring period, such as a calendar year.

To perform this function, follow the menu path:

MENU PATH: SAP REFERENCE IMG • ENVIRONMENT, HEALTH AND SAFETY • PRODUCT SAFETY • SUBSTANCE VOLUME TRACKING • CLICK SPECIFY DATA TRANSFER (PROPERTY TREE)

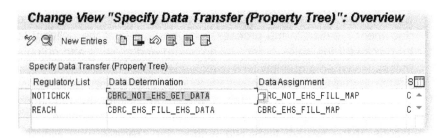

Figure 2.51: Specify data transfer property tree

Step 6: Specify regulatory lists

In this step, create the regulatory lists you require, e.g., substance lists (see Figure 2.52). By assigning a regulatory list to an identifier, you specify the regulatory list to which the identifier belongs or from which the identifier was taken. An identifier can relate to several regulatory lists. However, in a special case, one specification can occur under several different identifiers in the same regulatory list. For example, there are specifications that are entered several times in the CAS library under different CAS numbers (see Figure 2.53).

To perform this function, follow the menu path:

MENU PATH: SAP REFERENCE IMG • ENVIRONMENT, HEALTH AND SAFETY • BASIC DATA AND TOOLS • SPECIFICATION MANAGEMENT • SPECIFICATION MASTER • SPECIFY REGULATORY LISTS.

Entries for regulatory lists that have already been used in the production system must not be deleted. You can also enter regulatory lists in BASIC DATA and TOOLS. For more information, see the SAP Library for the component basic data and tools under regulatory list management.

Step 6 completes the ECC configuration steps. In the next section, we will move on to the SAP GTS configurations steps to enable the compliance check for EH&S.

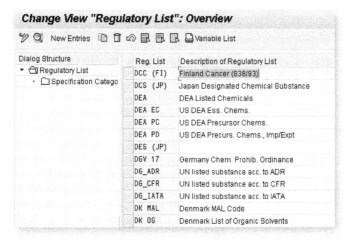

Figure 2.52: Regulatory list overview´

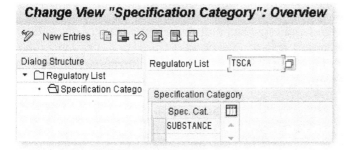

Figure 2.53: Specification category in the regulatory list

2.8.4   GTS configurations for EH&S

Let's now walk through the configuration steps for the EH&S set up in SAP GTS.

Step 1: Define legal regulations

In this step, define a legal regulation for the hazardous substance check (see Figure 2.54). The menu path is SAP GLOBAL TRADE SERVICES • GENERAL SETTINGS • LEGAL REGULATIONS • DEFINE LEGAL REGULATIONS.

Figure 2.54: Define legal regulations

Within the TYPE OF LEGAL CODE, select PROHIBITION AND RESTRICTION from the drop-down menu and select IMPORT/ARRIVAL AND EX-PORT/DISPATCH from the IMPORT/EXPORT indicator. Key in the original country of legal regulation.

Step 2: Activate the legal regulations at the country/country group level (see Figure 2.55). In this screen, you need to list all of the countries that you are exporting from and importing to, and the hazardous substance check will be performed with the logistics documents (sales order, purchase order, etc.).

The menu path is SAP GLOBAL TRADE SERVICES • GENERAL SETTINGS • LEGAL REGULATIONS • ACTIVATE LEGAL REGULATIONS AT COUNTRY/COUNTRY GROUP LEVEL.

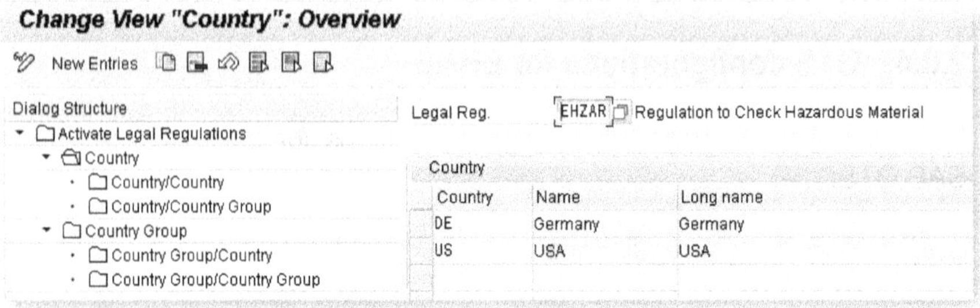

Figure 2.55: Activate legal regulation

Step 3: Define the determination procedure for active legal regulations (see Figure 2.56).

In Step 3, specify which determination procedure the system should use to determine the active legal regulation in the hazardous substance check service. The determination procedure contains the rules that the system uses to determine the active legal regulation.

The menu path is SAP GLOBAL TRADE SERVICES • GENERAL SETTINGS • LEGAL REGULATIONS • ACTIVATE LEGAL REGULATIONS AT COUNTRY/COUNTRY GROUP LEVEL.

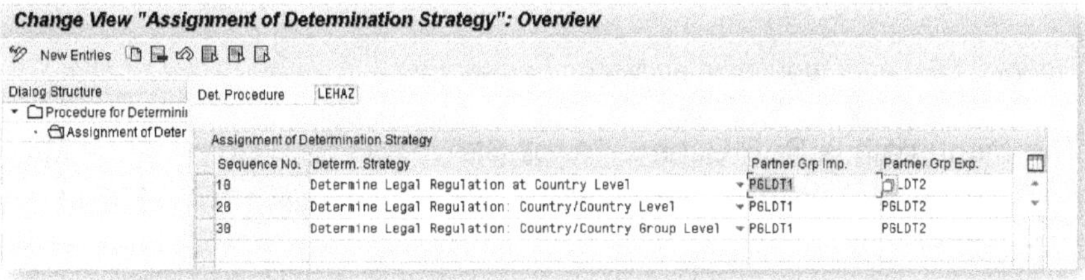

Figure 2.56: Determination strategy assignment

Step 4: Assign the determination procedure for active legal regulations (see Figure 2.57).

Following the definition of the determination of the procedure, we need to assign it to the hazardous substance check to determine active legal regulation. This will help the system determine the legal regulation based on the procedure defined in the earlier step.

The menu path is SAP GLOBAL TRADE SERVICES • SAP COMPLIANCE MANAGEMENT • "HAZARDOUS SUBSTANCE CHECK" SERVICE • ASSIGN DETERMINATION PROCEDURE FOR ACTIVE LEGAL REGULATION.

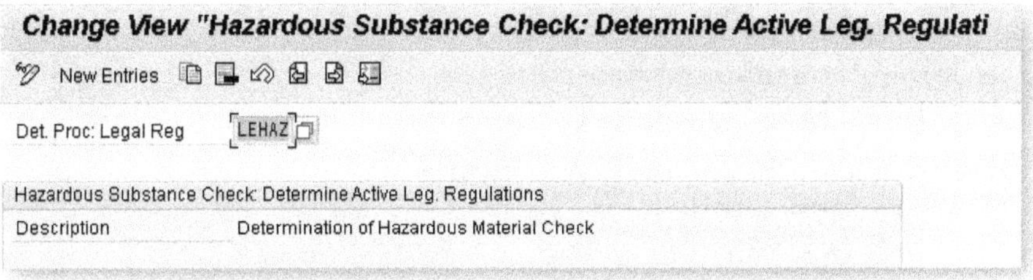

Figure 2.57: Hazardous substance check assignment

Step 5: Activate legal regulations. Based on the countries you defined in Step 2, the import or export check for hazardous substance check service needs to be activated (see Figure 2.58). Select CHECK: DIS-

157

PATCH/EXPORT INCLUDING DOMESTIC to check for export transaction and domestic transactions.

Figure 2.58: Legal regulation activation by country

The menu path is SAP GLOBAL TRADE SERVICES • SAP COMPLIANCE MANAGEMENT • "HAZARDOUS SUBSTANCE CHECK" SERVICE • ACTIVATE LEGAL REGULATION.

Step 5: Define control data for hazardous substance check service (see Figure 2.59). This step allows you to activate the hazardous substance check for the legal regulation defined in Step 1 by checking the box HAZ. SUBS CHECK ACTIVE and partner functions for export within the PARTNER GROUP TO DETERMINE COUNTRY OF DESTINATION and for import within the PARTNER GROUP TO DETERMINE COUNTRY OF DEPARTURE areas.

The menu path is SAP GLOBAL TRADE SERVICES • SAP COMPLIANCE MANAGEMENT • "HAZARDOUS SUBSTANCE CHECK" SERVICE • CONTROL DATA FOR HAZARDOUS SUBSTANCE CHECK SERVICE.

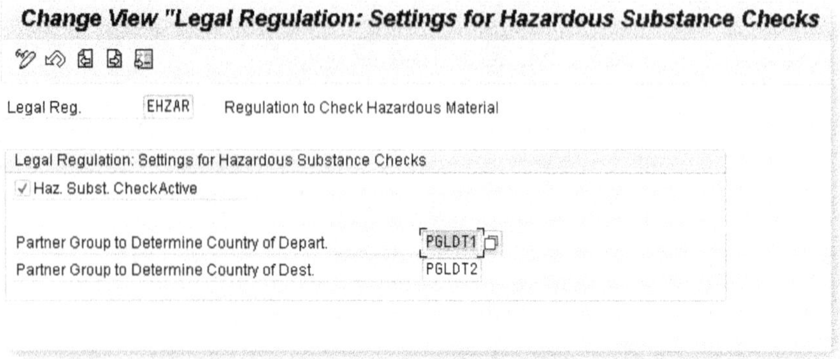

Figure 2.59: Control settings for hazardous substance checks

Optional Step 6: Define alternative RFC destination for SAP ERP EH&S (see Figure 2.60).

158

The hazardous substance check uses functions in SAP SAP EH&S from SAP ERP to perform the checks for business transactions in SAP GTS. If you have installed your SAP ERP EH&S on a different system than your feeder system, you must configure IMG activity to specify the RFC destination where SAP GTS can call the hazardous substance check in SAP ERP EH&S.

Choose the logical system from which you transfer the logistics documents and assign it the RFC destination for the SAP ERP EH&S system.

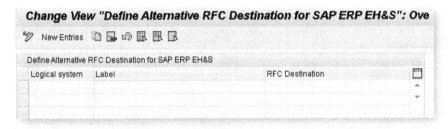

Figure 2.60: Define alternative RFC festination for ERP

Once you complete the configuration steps above, when you create a sales order, delivery note, or purchase order, it creates a customs document within compliance management and performs the hazardous service check as shown in Figure 2.61. If the check fails, then it will have a red block indicator.

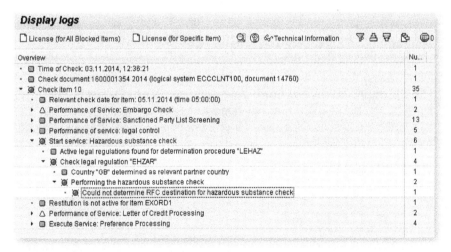

Figure 2.61: Hazardous substance compliance check in GTS

2.9 Examples of daily user functions in compliance

This section reviews several common daily user functions in the GTS compliance area. This list is not meant to be a comprehensive review of all available functions; rather, these activities have been identified as commonly used and illustrate how to use the system.

2.9.1 Legal control – export

All of the functions in Section 2.9.1 can be reached through the GTS cockpit by clicking on the LEGAL CONTROL – EXPORT button (see Figure 2.62).

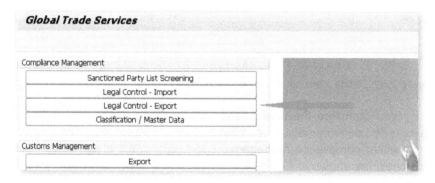

Figure 2.62: Legal control—export

Monitoring—display blocked documents

When you enter this function, you are faced with a large menu. You can use this menu to narrow down your searches by many fields and functions. If you choose, you do not need to select or identify anything, and can leave the results wide open. If you do, you will see all blocked documents and whether they are blocked for:

- ▶ Missing data or other status issue
- ▶ Embargo
- ▶ SPL
- ▶ Export control
- ▶ Hazmat check
- ▶ Restitution
- ▶ Letter of credit

You can choose to view only those documents that blocked for a specific reason or multiple reasons. You can also narrow your search by:

▶ FTO

▶ Legal unit

▶ Legal regulation

▶ Year

▶ Date

▶ Document number

Regardless of the selection you make, you will be taken to a results screen (see the example in Figure 2.63).

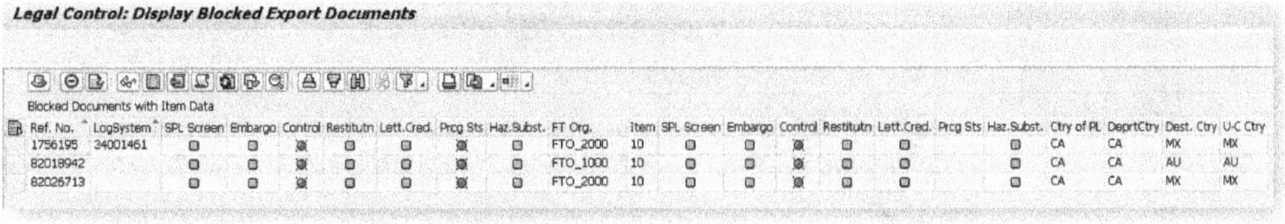

Figure 2.63: Display blocked export documents

This is a very useful screen to review documents and provides a snapshot of the blocks currently in the system. It is not, however, a comprehensive tool for releasing or dealing with these documents. If the block is for a reason such as SPL, restitution, or embargo, you will need to back out and go to those specific areas to deal with the issue. Similarly, if the block is due to missing data, you will have to correct the data. If, on the other hand, the block is due to an export control license requirement, it can be dealt with right in this screen if certain conditions are met. Two possible scenarios are described below.

Scenario 1: Release the document by assigning it to a license.

If the document is blocked due to a license requirement, you can release the document in this screen by assigning the document to a license. This assumes, of course, that the license is already set up. If no suitable license has been set up, you cannot resolve the issue in this area alone.

Provided the license exists, you can highlight your document and click on the CHANGE CONTROL DATA BUTTON 🔲.

This will take you to a screen that lists all of the available licenses and you can assign your document to one. This illustrates the principle explained in Section 2.10.4 where the same user who creates licenses is not necessarily the one who uses them. Using this logic, you could only provide certain users access to this function in GTS (view documents and assign licenses) and provide a different user exclusive access to creating licenses.

Scenario 2: Release the document by changing the product classification

---

Be very careful with classification changes

 This scenario is one that should not be used unless the user is a compliance specialist who clearly understands the legal requirements. If the classification is wrong, then this may be an appropriate approach. If, however, the user is wrongfully changing the classification just to release the document, you could end up in serious trouble.

The other way to release a blocked document in the review blocked documents screen is to change the classification of the product. Let's look at the scenario.

The user has entered the DISPLAY BLOCKED EXPORT DOCUMENTS screen (see Figure 2.63) and sees that a document is blocked for a license check. When they click on the DISPLAY BLOCKED REGULATION button (⊝), they see the reason for this block. In this case, the reason is that classification 7-3.6.m to Mexico requires a license under the Canadian Export Controls (EARCA) regulation (see Figure 2.64).

Legal Control: Display Blocked Export Documents

Ref. No.	LogSystem	SPL Screen	Embargo	Control	Restitutn	Lett.Cred.	Prcg Sts	Haz.Subst.	FT Org.	Item	SPL Screen	Embargo	Control	Restitutn	Lett.Cred.	Prcg Sts	Haz.Subst.	Ctry of PL	DeprtCtry	Dest. Ctry	U-C Ctry
1756195	34001461			▨			▨		FTO_2000	10			▨					CA	CA	MX	MX
82018942				▨			▨		FTO_1000	10			▨					CA	CA	AU	AU
82026713				▨			▨		FTO_2000	10			▨					CA	CA	MX	MX

Ref. No. LogSystem Item L.Reg. Number Grouping
1756195 34001461 10 EARCA 7-3.6.m

Figure 2.64: Display legal regulation causing block

At this point, the user could change the classification of the product if they know that 7-3.6.m is incorrect. As warned, this must not be done unless the user is certain that he or she is making the correct, compliant choice. To do so, click on the CHANGE PRODUCT MASTER button (⚙) and adjust the classification. Once this step is complete, click on the PERFORM NEW CHECK button (⚙).

We cannot state enough that this function must be used with caution. We recommend that you restrict access to this function to prevent errors. In fact, we mention the function here more as a warning rather than as a suggestion. Now that you are aware of this function, you can prevent its misuse.

Export licenses – Create/maintain export licenses

The MAINTAIN EXPORT LICENSES function has three options: create, change, and display ☐ ✎ ✂.

When you create a license, you will be taken to the menu shown in Figure 2.65 that allows you to choose the LEGAL REGULATION and LICENSE TYPE. Furthermore, you can select an existing license to use as a template.

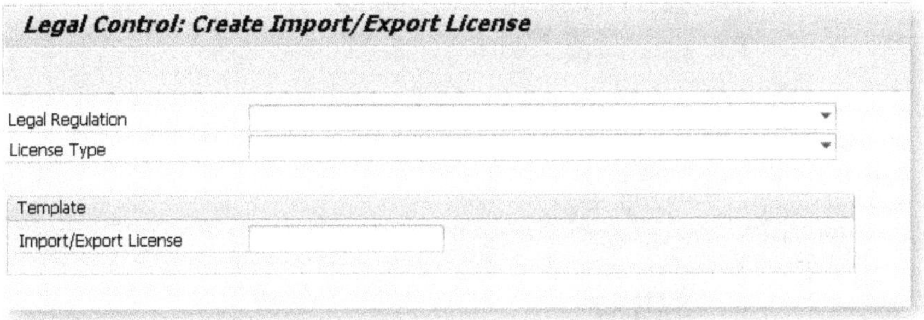

Legal Control: Create Import/Export License

Legal Regulation	▼
License Type	▼
Template	
Import/Export License	

Figure 2.65: Create license menu

Once you have made your selections, you will be taken to the main license screen (see Figure 2.66). There are several functions here; some of the key ones are described below are the essential fields that will decide whether your license is compliant or not. Please also see Section 2.10.1 for more information on compliant license creation and use.

Actual government issued license vs. internal controls

 As has been discussed elsewhere, GTS license functionality can be used with government-issued licenses and permits, as well as with internal controls not mandated by a regulatory body. The discussion below assumes that you have a government issued license. It is absolutely critical that you enter the contents of that license into GTS accurately!

Legal Control: Create Import/Export License

General Data

Legal Regulation	EAR	Export Administration Regulations
License Type	VL	Validated License
Import/Export License	20000000000000000001	
External Number		
Valid From		To

Attributes with Multip...
- Status
- Quants
- Doc. Numbers
- Texts
- Administr.

Status

Activ	Icon	Status	Created on	Time	Comment
●	☐	License Created	01/31/2015	12:03:04	
○		License Application...		00:00:00	
○		License Application...		00:00:00	
○		License Active		00:00:00	
○		License Submitted f...		00:00:00	
○		License Expired		00:00:00	
○				00:00:00	

Attributes

Foreign Trade Org. Unit	
Country of Dept./Dest.	
External Product ID	
Logical System Group	
Control Class	

Figure 2.66: License screen

EXTERNAL NUMBER: This must be the actual license number given to you by the government. It will appear on critical GTS-generated documents and communications, such as the export declaration.

VALID FROM: Ensure this value matches the dates exactly provided to you by the government. Most licenses cover a specific period of time, and GTS needs to know this.

QUANTS (QUANTITIES): This must be the exact quantity shown on your government license. For example, if they allow you to export 1000 liters of a particular chemical under the license, you must capture that here.

Quantities in licenses

 Check the unit of measure used in your product SKU and compare it to the unit of measure used in the government-issued license. For example, you may measure your product in SAP using "EA" (each), and the product is a five-gallon pail containing 18.9 liters. Your license allows 1000 liters of product to be exported. The quantity you will want to capture in GTS is 52 EA. This will be the most you can export without exceeding 1000 liters.

FOREIGN TRADE ORG. UNIT: This is critical: your license will belong to and be useful for a specific legal entity. Ensure sure that GTS knows which legal entity is allowed to use the license. Your company may represent multiple legal entities acting as a business group, but the license will be specific to one or more of them. Make sure you do not accidentally violate the terms of the license by improperly setting up FTO.

COUNTRY OF DEPT./DEST.: Enter the allowed country of departure or destination in this field. This will be the country you plan to trade with. For example, if your chosen FTO is in the US, this is the country you plan to sell to. You do not need to confirm the US because it is attached to the FTO. If the license is for exports to Mexico, you would enter MX.

CONTROL CLASS: Enter the ECCN or other classification number tied to the license in this field. For example, if your license is from the BIS to export 1C350.3.a-classified items to Mexico, you would enter that classification here.

This should wrap up your license creation stage. At some point, you will return to edit the license and assign a document or documents to it. Alternatively, the document assignation may happen in the DISPLAY BLOCKED DOCUMENTS screen as described above.

Embargo—release blocked documents

The menu for EMBARGO – RELEASE BLOCKED DOCUMENTS is quite large and allows you to filter/narrow it down by multiple factors such as:

- ▶ Legal regulation
- ▶ FTO
- ▶ Document number
- ▶ Date

If you are like most operations, you will be able to run this report without restrictions because embargo blocks are rare. However, depending on the unique needs of your organization, this may be a menu you need to spend more time on. Once you have made your choices, the results screen appears (see Figure 2.67).

Figure 2.67: Release blocked export documents (embargo)

On this screen, you can review all documents currently blocked due to an embargo. You can also release them.

Be careful with embargo release

You must question why you would ever release an embargo block! If the embargo is legitimate, then you likely are forbidden to transact with that country. Be very careful here.

To release the document, highlight it and click on the CANCEL EMBARGO BLOCK button (). You will be asked if you are sure to double-check. Click on YES and you will go to the REASONS FOR RELEASE dialogue. Similar to the same function in SPL, you can choose a predefined reason and add notes or text to it.

As we will discuss in the compliance tips section (see Section 2.10), we recommend that you use licenses in situations where an embargo is not absolute. If you must release documents in the embargo screen, ensure that your compliance manager runs the ANALYZE REASONS FOR RELEASE report regularly as part of an audit program.

Embargo—analyze reasons for release

Analyze reasons for release is a reporting tool that should be part of your audit program (see Section 2.10.5). Using this functionality, you can see all user decisions to release an embargo-blocked document. You will also see the reason they chose at the time of release.

You will need to activate the catalog of reasons for release, or this function will not work. If this is the case, you will see an error message like the one shown in Figure 2.68. For this reason, it is essential that you activate these reasons in configuration. Otherwise, you will be missing a critical audit tool.

Figure 2.68: Reason for release not active

2.9.2   Legal control – import

In this section, we will walk you through the import set up for inward and inbound movements. To access LEGAL CONTROL – IMPORT, click on the button with the same name in the GTS Cockpit menu (see Figure 2.69).

Global Trade Services

Compliance Management

> Sanctioned Party List Screening

> Legal Control - Import

> Legal Control - Export

> Classification / Master Data

Customs Management

> Export

Figure 2.69: Legal control—import

See Section 2.9.1 for a discussion of these functions from an export perspective. The import function is identical. LEGAL CONTROL IMPORT and LEGAL CONTROL EXPORT are very similar functions, but one focuses on purchase orders and other inbound documents, while the other focuses on orders and other outbound documents.

2.9.3 Compliance management: Classification/master data

All of the functions in Section 2.9.3 are accessed through the CLASSIFICATION / MASTER DATA button in the GTS Cockpit menu (see Figure 2.70). There are many functions in this section, but we will focus on the classification of products. We will describe and compare the two key methods for classification (individually and worklist) and then describe a reporting/analysis tool.

Harmonized tariff numbers vs. export control numbers

The process for classification is very similar whether you are classifying an HS number or an ECCN number. This section will focus on ECCN because it is the compliance chapter. See the customs management chapter in the sequel to this book for more detail on HS number classification.

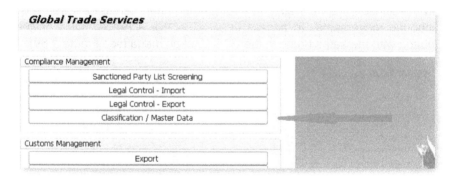

Figure 2.70: Classification/master data

Classify via worklist

On the CLASSIFICATION/MASTER DATA screen, you will find CLASSIFY VIA WORKLIST. This is a useful tool for classifying multiple products at once and can save time. However, it does not have the auditing tools that individual maintenance has.

When you click on this function, you will be taken to the CLASSIFY PRODUCTS VIS WORKLIST menu (see Figure 2.71). The options in this menu define the worklist that you will see when you click on EXECUTE. Let's walk through some key options and fields on this screen.

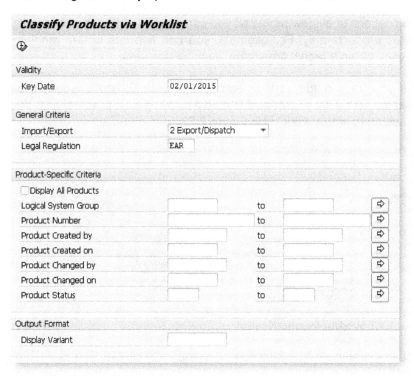

Figure 2.71: Classify products via the worklist menu

IMPORT/EXPORT: Toggles between import control classifications and export control.

LEGAL REGULATION: Select an active legal regulation from the IMPORT/ EXPORT dropdown menu. The example in Figure 2.71 shows EX- PORT/DISPATCH, EAR.

DISPLAY ALL PRODUCTS: Check this option to see products that are already classified, or leave it blank to see only products not yet classified.

PRODUCT NUMBER: This can be a single product, a string of products, or a range. You can also enter a partial product code followed by an asterisk to see all codes that begin with that partial code.

PRODUCT CREATED ON: If your company is disciplined and maintains classifications of all new products, you can use this option to see recently created products only. For example, you can use this to see products classified within a recent timeframe, such as last week.

Once you have made your selections and click EXECUTE, you will be presented with a list of products filtered according to your selections. You can see an example work list in Figure 2.72.

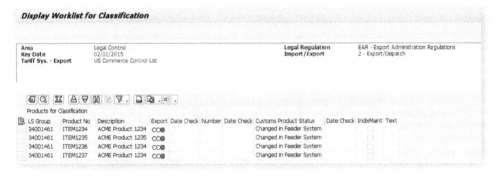

Figure 2.72: Worklist for classification

Once in the DISPLAY WORKLIST FOR CLASSIFICATION screen, you can classify products individually or as a group. The real power of this screen is to do so as a group. If you only need to classify one product, we recommend that you see the following section on individual maintenance.

To classify multiple products, highlight the ones you want to include and then click on the CLASSIFY MULTIPLE PRODUCTS button (▦).

You will be taken to a screen where you can assign the classification to those selected products (see Figure 2.73). Simply enter the desired classification and click the ▦ button again. You will have classified as many products as selected in one action. You do not need to click save; it saves automatically.

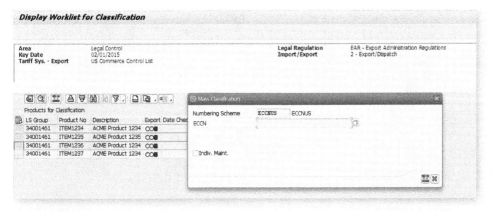

Figure 2.73: Assign multiple classifications

Maintain products

Unlike the CLASSIFY VIA WORKLIST option, this method forces you to classify products one at a time. However, it gives you some more auditing and commentary tools, which is preferable when you are performing sensitive classifications.

The menu options are more robust than in the worklist option, but in practice, you likely know the product code you seek. If not, and you need to search for it with these fields and options, there are some good tools available (e.g., dates, grouping, short text). For this exercise, we will assume that you are entering a single product code, as shown in Figure 2.74.

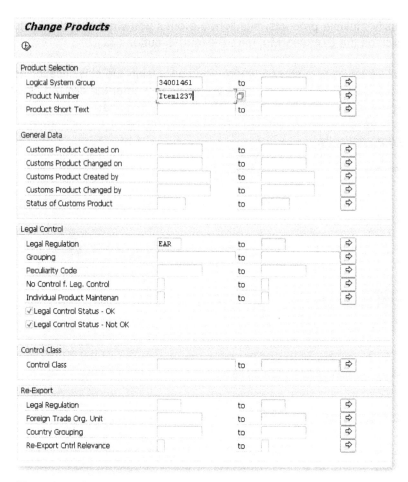

Figure 2.74: Change products menu

When you click EXECUTE, you will be go to a screen like the one in Figure 2.75. You will want to transfer to the LEGAL CONTROL tab to effect a classification as shown in Figure 2.76, in addition to the key activities available on this screen.

Change Products

⬚ Overview List On/Off   &

Product   ITEM1237   ACME Product 1234

| 🖥 General Basic Data | 🔒 Legal Control | 🕙 Prices & Values | 🔲 BOP |

General Data

Logical System Group	34001461	ECC Client 300
Internal Product No.	00000000000000100073	

Status	Changed in Feeder System	⬚ Flagged for Deletion						
Created by	RFC-GTS-ECC	On	02/01/2015	At	08:59:57	Time
Changed by	RFC-GTS-ECC	On	02/01/2015	At	08:59:58	Time

Basic Product Data

Base Unit	EA	Each			
Gross Weight	1.000		Weight Unit	LB	Pound
Net Weight	1.000				

Short Texts

Language	Description	
EN English	▾ ACME Product 1234	
	▾	
	▾	
	▾	

Units of Measure

X	AUn	Unit of...	<...	Y	BUn	Unit of...	Gross Weight	Net Weight	W...
1	EA	Each	<...	1	EA	Each		0.000	
			<...		EA	Each		0.000	
			<...		EA	Each		0.000	
			<...		EA	Each		0.000	
			<...		EA	Each		0.000	

Figure 2.75: Change products screen

173

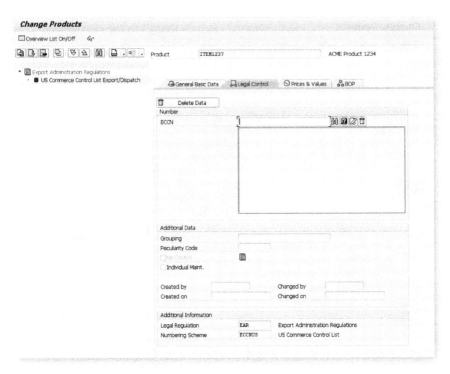

Figure 2.76: Legal control tab

ECCN: Choose and assign the classification for this product in this field. If you know it already, you can go ahead and enter it. If you are not sure, you can click on the FIND (📖) or CLASSIFICATION HELP (📖) buttons for assistance.

COMMENTS (📝). This is a useful tool where you can write a short comment. We advise getting into this habit when making sensitive classifications. For example, if you are classifying a chemical mixture containing Triethanolamine (TEA), you could state the exact percentage of TEA in the mixture so future auditors understand why you chose the classification you did.

ADD DOCUMENT (📑): This field is an even more powerful tool than the comments for audit trail purposes. You can upload a copy of any file or document you wish. Sticking with our TEA mixture example, you could upload a copy of the product formula or the MSDS. This will justify the reason for the classification should it ever be questioned or audited.

Once you have made your classification selection and added any desired documents or comments, click on SAVE, and you are finished.

Analyze product classification

This tool is found on the lower left side of the CLASSIFICATION/MASTER DATA menu.

This is a good tool for reviewing and auditing classification choices made by other users. It can also be useful for reviewing your own classifications made in the past. The menu screen allows you to pull up results by various options and filters such as (see Figure 2.77):

- ▶ Product number/range of numbers
- ▶ Product description
- ▶ Product created/changed on date
- ▶ Product created/changed by user
- ▶ Legal regulation
- ▶ Classification number

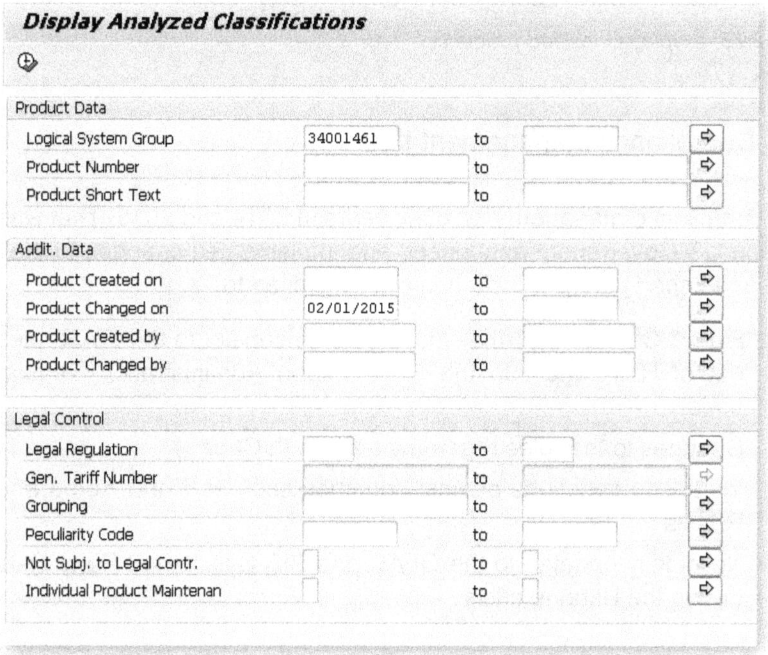

Display Analyzed Classifications

Product Data				
Logical System Group	34001461	to		⇨
Product Number		to		⇨
Product Short Text		to		⇨

Addit. Data				
Product Created on		to		⇨
Product Changed on	02/01/2015	to		⇨
Product Created by		to		⇨
Product Changed by		to		⇨

Legal Control				
Legal Regulation		to		⇨
Gen. Tariff Number		to		⇨
Grouping		to		⇨
Peculiarity Code		to		⇨
Not Subj. to Legal Contr.		to		⇨
Individual Product Maintenan		to		⇨

Figure 2.77: Display analyzed classifications

175

In our example, we are viewing all of the product classifications made on a given day. The results can be seen in Figure 2.78. In this example, we see several products and how they are classified over several legal regulations. As you can see, this is a powerful tool for reporting and auditing.

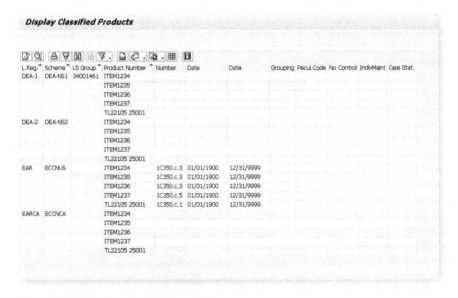

Figure 2.78: Display classified products

2.10   Compliance management tips

Trade compliance managers had busy years in 2014 and 2015. That was when the US Government announced and implemented changes to their export and import controls, including but not limited to:

▶ Export Control Reform – moving items subject to the ITAR rules out of ITAR and into the *EAR* (Export Administration Regulations)

▶ Changes to the rules regarding trade with Cuba

▶ Increased sanctions against countries such as North Korea and Russia

▶ Near-daily updates to the OFAC and BIS Sanctioned Party Lists during the Ukraine crisis.

Furthermore, UN and multinational efforts such as the Wassenaar Arrangement and Australia Group announced changes to their controlled products lists. This triggered changes to the export regulations in member countries.

These are challenging times for companies that trade internationally. More than ever, regulations regarding import and export controls seem to be a moving target. Thankfully, SAP GTS is a flexible, responsive tool that can adapt to these changes instantly, provided the administrators are on top of the required changes.

In the following section, we will go through some tips and suggestions for using SAP GTS to ensure that you are always compliant.

2.10.1 Export compliance tips

Classification of products (subscription)

The first thing you must decide regarding classification is whether to use a subscription service. There are third-party companies that will offer you the complete list of possible classifications for particular export control programs. This will ensure that you always have the most current and complete list available.

This decision should be based on the number of varying classifications you plan to use. Let us use the US ECCN (Export Control Classification Number) as an example. There are hundreds of ECCN numbers that may apply to your products, and they are subject to periodic changes/reforms. This would be a difficult list to maintain completely without a subscription.

If you know that you have only three or four different ECCN relevant to your product mix, then you probably do not require a complete list. Manually setting up a few classification numbers is not a significant job. However, if you have a product mix that consists of dozens of classifications, or if your mix frequently changes, you may need a subscription to ensure you always have the current ECCN list.

This is really a business decision; you can operate with or without a subscription in a compliant fashion. You have to weigh out the time cost of maintaining the data vs. the hard cost of the subscription price.

Licenses and license exceptions

SAP GTS makes a license decision based on the classification of the product and the country of destination. For example, if a US company were to enter an order for a customer in Russia for a product classified as 1C350, it would require a license, whereas that same product would not require a license for Canada.

On a basic level, this is how licenses work: when a requirement for a license is found, the document is blocked until you secure the appropriate license and enter in the data into SAP GTS.

Something to consider here is that most companies will limit the users who can set up a new license in GTS (See Section 2.10.4). Keep this in mind as you continue reading.

However, most regulatory bodies also have license exceptions. These are cases where a license is not required, despite the matching classification type and destination.

For example, US EAR allows a license exception for Tools of Trade (EAR 740.9(a)(1)) if they are going to be used by the shipper's employees in the destination country and either consumed or returned.

This raises two key questions:

1. How does GTS know if an exception applies?
2. How should this be handled in GTS?

The first question has a simple answer: GTS cannot possibly know this. A user will have to make the determination that the exception applies, which leads to the next answer.

The best way to handle this is to set up a license in advance for any exception you expect will apply to future shipments.

This will allow a user who has identified this exception to apply it to their document, without setting up a new license that could delay the shipment.

You can use a specific license type for these, such as EXCPT. This will make it clear to users and auditors that it is not an actual license but rather an exception.

We further recommend that you cite the license exception and make it clear that this is not an actual license. If you are audited later, internally or externally, it is important that this is clear and obvious so that the auditors can trust your system.

Figure 2.79 is a sample image of a license built to allow for the use of a license exception.

Figure 2.79: License exception example

Embargoes vs. license requirements

SAP GTS has embargo functionality that blocks all documents to or from a listed country. A common use for this is when US owned or based companies block all shipments to or from Cuba to comply with the Department of Treasury OFAC rules.

Most companies operate this way, and to ensure compliance, they simply forbid transactions with Cuba.

However, there are companies that do trade with Cuba and do so legally using licenses or license exceptions. In late 2014, the US announced more robust licenses and exceptions, which will only increase the number of the companies in the US that trade with Cuba. How will they manage this if Cuba is listed as an embargoed destination?

SAP GTS does have a release function for embargos, as shown in Figure 2.80.

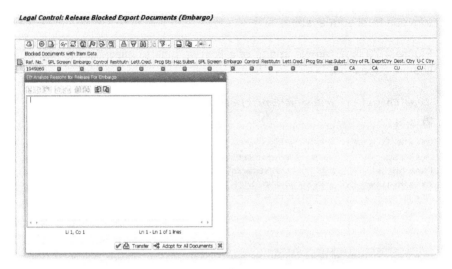

Figure 2.80: Release document (embargo)

However, this is not a very good system for audit purposes, as it only allows a simple text field explaining the purpose of the release.

If you are a company that plans to take advantage of US licenses and exceptions to Cuba, then we recommend the following approach. Of course, this scenario can apply in any country related to any embargoed destination, but we are using US/Cuba to illustrate.

First, remove Cuba from the list of embargoed countries. See Section 2.4 for a discussion of this process.

Next, create a control in GTS that **all** classifications of product require a license to Cuba.

Typically, licenses are required for specific ECCN/country combinations. Many ECCN classifications can export to most countries without a license. For this scenario, a license requirement will need to apply, regardless of classification, when the country is Cuba. Either this can be done by assigning all available classifications to the license determination or by creating an ECCN grouping that contains all ECCN within it.

This will cause all documents to Cuba to be held for a license check and allow the user to determine if this is a valid use of a license and/or exception. This way, a proper audit trail will exist, and it will be a more transparent process than simply releasing the embargo on the document.

Reexport concerns

SAP GTS has robust re-export functionality. This allows you to maintain control after it leaves your original country, provided the business in the destination country is also on SAP GTS.

This kind of *extraterritorial control* is found in multiple US rules. For explanation purposes, we will use the EAR.

The US EAR rules extend control of products outside of the territory of the USA. This can even be true if the US origin product is transformed or consumed into a new product in the second country. As a result, that second country may require a US re-export license when they ship that newly created good (that contained US content).

If the second country simply re-ships the US origin good in the same condition, it will absolutely be controlled.

Figure 2.81 is an image taken from the EAR regulations 15 CFR 736.2(b)(1). This explains that both exports and re-exports may require a license. This leads to the question, what is a re-export? The Bureau of Industry and Security (BIS), which governs the EAR, offers some explanatory material on its website (see Figure 2.82)[2]. Figure 2.83 and Figure 2.84 are from the same website and explain when a license may be needed for a re-export.

(1) *General Prohibition One—Export and reexport of controlled items to listed countries (Exports and Reexports).* You may not, without a license or License Exception, export any item subject to the EAR to another country or reexport any item of U.S.-origin if each of the following is true:

(i) The item is controlled for a reason indicated in the applicable Export Control Classification Number (ECCN), and

(ii) Export to the country of destination requires a license for the control reason as indicated on the Country Chart at part 738 of the EAR. (The scope of this prohibition is determined by the correct classification of your item and the ultimate destination as that combination is reflected on the Country Chart.)[1] Note that each License Exception described at part 740 of the EAR supersedes General Prohibition One if all terms and conditions of a given License Exception are met by the exporter or reexporter.

Figure 2.81: EAR 736.2(b)(1)

---

[2] "Guidance on the Commerce Department's Reexport Controls", accessed July 7, 2015, http://www.bis.doc.gov/index.php/forms-documents/doc_view/4-guidelines-to-reexport-publications

What is a Reexport?

A *reexport* is the shipment or transmission of an item subject to the EAR from one foreign country (i.e., a country other than the United States) to another foreign country. A reexport also occurs when there is "release" of technology or software (source code) subject to the EAR in one foreign country to a national of another foreign country.

Figure 2.82: BIS—What is a re-export?

A. Determining whether a U.S.-origin item requires a license from BIS.

You may need to obtain a license to "reexport" an item that was produced or originated in the United States. Many items subject to the EAR do not need a license to be reexported from one foreign country to another. But certain items are controlled and will either require a license or must qualify for a License Exception.

Figure 2.83: US origin item may need license

B. Determining whether your foreign-produced product requires a license from BIS because it contains some U.S.-origin content.

As noted above, certain foreign-produced items are also subject to the EAR because they contain more than a specified percentage value of U.S.-origin controlled content. You need to first determine if your foreign produced item is subject to the EAR. If you determine your foreign produced item is subject to the EAR, you will then follow the process outlined in Part A above to determine if your foreign-produced item requires a license.

Figure 2.84: Foreign produced product may require a license

Let's walk through a simple process flow to illustrate how this may look. Figure 2.85 represents a US company exporting a product to its Canadian subsidiary. The Canadian subsidiary later re-exports that product to Russia. Remember, even if the Canadian company uses the US product to manufacture a completely new Canadian origin product, the re-export could still require a license. GTS allows you to construct these rules and will actually check the Bill of Material in the Canadian system to look for controlled US product. For ease of illustration, in this example the product is re-exported without changes.

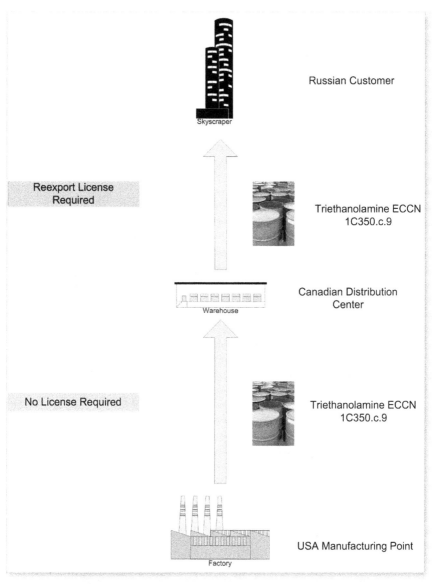

Russian Customer

Reexport License
Required

Triethanolamine ECCN
1C350.c.9

Canadian Distribution
Center

No License Required

Triethanolamine ECCN
1C350.c.9

USA Manufacturing Point

Figure 2.85: Re-export flow

You may notice that no license is required when the product ships from the USA to Canada, but a license is required when that same product ships from Canada to Russia. This raises a very serious area of risk for many North American companies.

Canada enjoys a privileged status with US regulatory bodies, such as the Department of Commerce. Very few products require a license when they ship from the US to Canada. Figure 2.86 shows what is called the Commerce Country Chart – Supplement No. 1 to Part 738 of EAR. If there is an "X" in the column, then a license is required when items of that category ship to that country. As you can see, very little requires a license to Canada, as opposed to other countries.

Commerce Control List Overview and the Country Chart — Supplement No. 1 to Part 738 page 3

Commerce Country Chart

Reason for Control

Countries	Chemical & Biological Weapons			Nuclear Nonproliferation		National Security		Missile Tech	Regional Stability		Firearms Convention	Crime Control			Anti-Terrorism	
	CB 1	CB 2	CB 3	NP 1	NP 2	NS 1	NS 2	MT 1	RS 1	RS 2	FC 1	CC 1	CC 2	CC 3	AT 1	AT 2
Bulgaria[3]	X			X		X		X	X							
Burkina Faso	X	X		X		X	X	X	X	X		X			X	
Burma	X	X	X	X		X	X	X	X	X		X			X	
Burundi	X	X		X		X	X	X	X	X		X			X	
Cambodia	X	X		X		X	X	X	X	X		X	X			
Cameroon	X	X		X		X	X	X	X	X		X			X	
Canada	X										X					
Cape Verde	X	X		X		X	X	X	X	X		X			X	
Central African Republic	X	X		X		X	X	X	X	X		X			X	
Chad	X	X		X		X	X	X	X	X		X			X	
Chile	X	X		X		X	X	X	X	X	X	X			X	
China	X	X	X	X		X	X	X	X	X		X			X	
Colombia	X	X		X		X	X	X	X	X	X	X			X	

Export Administration Regulations — Bureau of Industry and Security — December 23, 2014

Figure 2.86: Commerce country chart

Because of this, there is a real danger for companies that operate primarily within the US and Canadian markets. They can fall into a pattern of never needing an export license because their trade is between the US and Canada, and no license is required. They may be caught unaware if, at some point, they open up business in new countries and begin exporting from Canada to those countries. They may not realize they are breaking US law because they were not educated or prepared for this.

Properly setting up GTS will protect your company and block shipments as necessary, whether this happens weekly for you or if it comes up once in ten years. When you do run into it, GTS will be ready, unlike a manual system.

2.10.2 Import compliance tips

Embargoes vs. license requirements

In Section 2.10.1 we discussed the use of embargo vs. license for a scenario when a US company exports to Cuba. The same situation can apply in an import scenario. While the previous discussion focused on exports, it is equally applicable to imports.

Using import licenses to manage quantity limits, substance lists, and quotas

Many countries have rules regarding how much of a given product can be imported. These rules can come from a variety of sources:

- ▶ Textile quotas
- ▶ Agricultural quotas
- ▶ Chemical inventories
- ▶ Other controlled products or chemicals (e.g., drug precursors controlled by the DEA in the US)

These rules are not truly a license requirement. If you import a quantity within the allowance, you are not required to report your activity. However, you must not import more than the permitted quantity. As an example, we will use the Canadian Domestic Substance List (DSL), which governs the import of chemicals new to the Canadian market.

If a chemical is on the DSL list, then it is considered part of the Canadian marketplace already. In other words, people are already making, importing, and/or using this chemical. If this is the case, there is no limit on how much you can import.

If, however, the product is not on the DSL list, then you face a more difficult scenario. Generally, you can import up to 1,000 KG of the product without any permit or notification requirement, but you must not import more than that without contacting Environment Canada.

There are then progressive stages of notification after that as you progress up to 10,000 KG and beyond.

How can you be sure you do not exceed these limits if you have identified a non-DSL product?

SAP GTS can help with this. You can set up an import license requirement for those products into Canada.

You can prearrange a standing 1,000 KG license, allowing GTS users to import up to that amount by assigning their documents to the license. Once they exceed that limit, their documents will be blocked until someone creates a new license in GTS. This will not be done until the required notification to Environment Canada has been made to allow import of up to 10,000 KG.

Since you will have separated user roles appropriately (see Section 2.10.4), this will allow the business to operate without interruption until you reach the limits.

This is a way you can use SAP GTS import license functionality to ensure compliance of a non-license, quota-type regulation. As you review the countries you operate in, you will likely find many more scenarios like this where SAP GTS can help.

2.10.3 Classification compliance tips

Schedule B vs. HTS USA

The US maintains two separate versions of the Harmonized Tariff Schedule. One is called the *Harmonized Tariff Schedule of the United States (HTS US)* and is primarily intended for imports into the US. It has also been historically referred to as the Schedule A list. It is administered by the US International Trade Administration Commission (*USITC*).

The other is called the *Schedule B*. It is administered by the US Census Bureau, Foreign Trade Division. This list is intended for reporting exports from the USA.

Many companies report their imports using the HTS US and their exports using the Schedule B.

When you implement GTS, assuming you intend to use both import and export functionality, you will need to decide whether to maintain both lists.

It is an ideal situation that you maintain only the HTS US list and use it for both exports and imports. This will save time and energy, as only one list must be updated and loaded.

This is perfectly legal according to 15 CFR 30.6(a)(12), which states that you can either report either the Schedule B classification or the HTS US, with some exceptions (found in the "head note of the HTS US").

These exceptions are found in the Notice to Exporters section of the HTS US. Be sure to review this notice; it is a 12-page list of goods that cannot be reported for export using HTS US, but must use Schedule B. The list can be found here:

http://www.usitc.gov/publications/docs/tata/hts/bychapter/1500n2x.pdf

Provided you do not have any of these products, you should be able to use the HTS US for both imports and exports, saving a great deal of time and cost.

ECCN classification tips

The following discussion will focus on the US EAR ECCN system, but the same points can apply to any classification-based trade control system, such as:

▶ US Department of State ITAR Classifications
▶ Canadian Foreign Affairs Export Control List
▶ Australian Defense and Strategic Goods List
▶ Countless other country control lists

For explanatory purposes, we will specifically only look at the ECCN system.

The US Department of Commerce is responsible for the Commerce and Foreign Trade Regulations, specifically 15 CFR 730-799. These are known as the Export Administration Regulations (EAR).

These regulations create a complicated system of classification of products. This is known as the Export Control Classification Number, or ECCN. The list they are maintained in is the Commerce Control List (CCL).

This classification is critical, as it drives the possible requirement for an export license, as well as various other regulatory mandates such as reporting.

SAP GTS, as has been discussed in this chapter, is a tool to ensure that you properly manage your ECCN-classified products. Once you set up the ECCN for a specific material master, you can use GTS to ensure you never fail to secure a license through document blocking.

However, GTS is a tool for managing products with an ECCN assigned; it cannot help with your ECCN classification process.

Here are some recommendations for your ECCN process, which will help ensure that you have a compliant system in place. Should you ever be audited by the US Department of Commerce, taking these steps will go a long way to ensure a positive result.

ECCN Tip 1: Find expertise in your business sector

 The CCL consists of many different products, ranging from obscure chemicals with names dozens of letters long to body armor, software, and infrared cameras! As a result, not very many people are "experts" in using the whole CCL. Someone who works in the chemical industry may be a specialist in those specific chemical controls, but will they know if your computer contains controlled encryption software? If you don't have the necessary expertise in-house, seek out third party assistance with specific CCL expertise related to your area of business. Do not pay a third party to classify your coated steel pipes if their specialty is rifle scopes.

ECCN Tip 2: Make ECCN classification a required part of new product set up

 The safest way to ensure proper classification of all your products is to require that all new product set-ups go through this step. If you allow new product set up to happen without it, on the assumption that "it will get done," you may find you have exported the good before you classified it and missed a critical license requirement. Do not allow new products in your system until they are classified.

ECCN Tip 3: Don't only look at currently exported products

The CCL is relevant to more than just exports. You can also violate the EAR by allowing a foreign national to view the plans for creating your CCL controlled product simply as having them in your factory for a tour! Similarly, the US Department of Commerce identifies some people in the US that require a license for controlled products, and even though you did not export it, they are deemed a high enough risk that a license is needed. You will not know how sensitive your items are until you classify them. Furthermore, you may export tomorrow what you sell domestically today—do not get caught unaware; classify everything!

ECCN Tip 4: Review past classifications regularly

Most manufacturing companies alter their formulas, plans, designs, etc. over time. In other words, the same product may be made slightly different today than it was last year. To give a chemical example, you may currently use Triethanolamine (TEA) in your chemical mixture, which triggers a 1C350 control, and you have set up the appropriate products in GTS with that classification. At some point, your R&D learns that an alternate to TEA is available, and they change the formula. Your product no longer requires the 1C350 classification; do you have internal systems that will catch this and make the required change? This can apply to other areas such as electronics. Imaging cameras are classified according to very precise specifications such as number of pixels and wavelengths. If you alter the specification, you could change the classification. For these reasons, it is essential that a product is not only reviewed once in its lifetime, but is also subject to periodic reviews.

ECCN Tip 5: Monitor changes To EAR and impact on your products

 Similarly to Tip 4, there is another reason mandating reviews of existing classifications. The classifications themselves can change over time. The US Department of Commerce periodically alters, edits, removes, and adds classifications. You need to be aware of these changes and review the impact on your existing classification decisions. GTS can help with outright classification additions and deletions, assuming you have a subscription service that will be updated. If you had previously classified a product, and that classification number no longer exists, GTS has tools to assist with this called re-classification. Sometimes, however, the Department of Commerce will not change the classification but rather the criteria within it. For example, in 2014, several toxins previously classified under 1C360 were moved to 1C351. You need to be responsive to these types of changes, which can only happen through regular reviews.

ECCN Tip 6: Take care not to assume EAR 99 – Product nature vs. use

 A common mistake made by companies during the classification stage is exclusively focusing on the content or material nature of their products. As a result, the company assumes their product is EAR99 (not controlled) simply because it is not specifically listed in the CCL. However, the use, purpose, or design of your product can also trigger a classification, and this is not always appreciated. The most commonly known use is the classification of goods "specially designed" for military use. However, less commonly understood purposes could place a good in a classification other than EAR99. For example, an otherwise EAR99 "harmless" item can become classified if it is "specially designed" for use with nuclear plants. Even paint could be classified, if it is designed specifically for use in a nuclear plant. This is the subject of an actual multimillion-dollar penalty that was in the news recently! Other things to watch for are products and equipment designed to operate at extreme depths or altitudes, temperatures, etc.

> ## ECCN Tip 7: Document your classification process
>
> Above all, document everything! All of your products should have a short file that describes the process that was used to determine classification. BIS considers robust compliance plans a mitigating factor should you be found in violation of a rule. In other words, having a robust plan and failing is better than never trying. It will have a material impact on penalties and enforcement. Documenting your formal classification process and the specific decision tree used on each product is an essential part of any compliance program.

2.10.4 User roles

Each company will have to develop a user role strategy that fits its business needs. There is no "canned" or out of the box solution for this, but we can make some suggestions and observations based on experience.

We have divided the various tasks from compliance into these broad categories:

1. Configuration/set up of GTS compliance.
2. Set up/maintenance of classification numbers.
3. Maintain determination strategy.
4. Classification of products.
5. Review/release blocked documents.
6. Create and maintain licenses.
7. Assign documents to licenses.

These seven categories can be further grouped:

- ▶ Configuration (#1)
- ▶ Periodic User Roles (#2&3)
- ▶ Master Data Maintenance (#4)
- ▶ Daily User Roles (#5-7)

The very first thing to consider when developing your strategy is the size and complexity of your organization. If, for example, you have 50 different products and average one license requirement a year, you can probably assign nearly all the roles to one person! If, on the other hand, you have thousands of products and require a license every week, the roles will need to be split up out of necessity as well as for compliance purposes.

Some suggestions related to each role group follow.

Configuration (#1)

Most companies follow the generally accepted best practice that configuration is kept separate from the user experience. IT or "SAP Specialists" generally have sole access to SAP GTS configuration, and the users who manage cockpit activities cannot go into configuration.

This is because the activities in configuration are critical and sensitive; misuse or an incorrect action can cause the entire system to fail. For this reason, we recommend that the individuals performing role categories 2-7 are not the same ones that perform role category 1.

Everything deemed "configuration" for the purpose of this discussion is found outside the GTS main menu, in the "SPRO – Customizing" section. All discussions after this (categories 2-7) refer to functions found in the "Main Menu," or cockpit section, of GTS.

Periodic user roles (2&3)

This category covers functions found in GTS that are performed infrequently and are very critical and/or sensitive. Improper use of these sections will cause GTS to be ineffective for your compliance needs.

Setting up and maintaining classification numbers can be done manually or through a subscription service. Either way, it is essential; it is one of the key drivers of license determination.

The other key driver in license determination is the determination strategy. This is where you tell the system which countries require a license for which classification type.

Due to the infrequency and sensitivity of this function, we recommend that this function fall with someone other than the daily users. This individual should be from the compliance part of your business, perhaps by a compliance manager or someone in a similar function. This way, all the changes made will be made by someone who appreciates the importance and meaning of what they are doing.

Master data maintenance (4)

There are as many ways to handle master data maintenance as there are types of master data! Bottom line? You need to trust that the data is accurate and complete. How you get there is up to you.

Specifically here we are referring to classification of products (e.g., setting them up with an ECCN number). An ideal best practice is one where the actual individual or individuals who make your classification determination are the same ones who set them up in GTS. This way, there is no chance of miscommunication. The individual setting up the classification in GTS is the one who decided what it should be.

This may not be realistic, of course. You may have a compliance manager determining classification who does not have time to set up each product. In this case, the compliance manager may need to hand the duty to a trusted subordinate or another GTS user. The classifications could be fed to the subordinate via email or a file. This is not as good of an approach, but it is the reality for many companies.

Daily user roles (5–7)

Lastly, we get to the heart of the compliance workload in GTS—reviewing blocked documents, setting up licenses, and assigning documents to licenses.

It can work perfectly fine to have users perform all of these roles, but we suggest one separation. Creating licenses and assigning documents should belong to a more limited number of users than the review of blocked documents.

Reviewing a blocked document is a fairly low-risk task by itself. The user will notice that a license is required and alert the necessary managers or experts. These experts should have exclusive rights to create a license and assign the document to it because this is the sensitive work.

Alternatively, if your company has many license requirements, you could restrict access to license creation but allow many users to assign documents to those licenses.

As previously stated, there are many way to develop a user role strategy. Just be sure you give yours adequate thought and planning and that it is a compliant, efficient model for you.

2.10.5 Auditing your compliance program

You will want to implement routine audits of your compliance system. There are multiple components and aspects to the system as discussed above, and due diligence requires you to audit its effectiveness. By "system," we do not simply mean "SAP GTS." We mean the comprehensive, total system around GTS, from configuration through subscription services to end user training. Figure 2.87 shows a high-level overview of the compliance chain. A weak link or break anywhere in this system could cause a failure and non-compliance. Each one of these sections must be audited periodically. After the diagram, are some ideas (not exhaustive) of areas to audit.

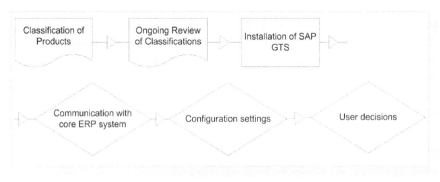

Figure 2.87: The compliance chain

Suggested areas to audit

Classification of products

▶ Are all products classified when a new product is set up?
▶ Who decides classification?
▶ Is the classification process documented?

Ongoing review of classifications

▶ Are all classified products reviewed periodically to see if the classification is still valid for that product?

▶ Are changes to the classification system implemented and the impact on your products reviewed?

Installation of SAP GTS

▶ Was SAP GTS installed properly and working as planned?

▶ Were all necessary aspects of compliance activated and defined?

Communication with the ERP system

▶ Are all necessary documents transferring to GTS for a compliance check?

▶ Are compliance blocks in GTS resulting in blocks in the ERP system?

▶ Are ERP users alerted to blocks when they occur?

Configuration settings

▶ Are the configuration settings right for your needs?

▶ Are the settings periodically reviewed and adjusted as needed?

▶ Do you periodically simulate a license requiring transaction and verify a positive result?

User Decisions

▶ Are licenses (past and present) audited for compliance to ensure user-performed licenses are set up appropriately?

▶ Do you test the license program, attempting to exceed quantity limits and recording result?

▶ Are user roles assigned according to strategy developed by compliance management?

3 SAP GTS Release 11.0

SAP released version 11.0 of GTS in early 2015, which is the latest version as of the writing of this book. SAP GTS 11.0 brings with it several key changes and enhancements, which we will summarize in this chapter. SAP GTS 11.0 includes changes to functionality not covered in the guide itself, so that the user has a full understanding of the difference between 11.0 and previous versions.

One of the key changes that 11.0 brings is compatibility with *SAP HANA*. SAP HANA is redefining database speed and capability in the SAP world with in-memory processing. It brings faster results on a larger scale for analytics, searches, and other functions that are typically limited by legacy systems. SAP GTS 11.0 is the first version to take advantage of HANA. As anyone who uses GTS can tell you, data searches, reports, and analytics are a big part of what GTS does. SAP HANA offers an opportunity to make GTS bigger and faster than ever before.

In addition to SAP HANA compatibility, 11.0 also brings with it some key new functionality. Some offer entirely new features, while others offer a simplified version of previously available features. Please read on to learn more about these new and simplified functions.

3.1 General configuration settings

There are some new selections and choices available in configuration to support new functionality. Let's review some of the new options and discuss their purpose and benefits. The features discussed in Section 3.1 are all found in the GENERAL SETTINGS portion of configuration.

3.1.1 Activate the SAP GTS Accelerator

The SAP GTS Accelerator is the tool in 11.0 that takes advantage of your HANA database. To activate it, follow the menu path SPRO • SAP REFERENCE IMG • GLOBAL TRADE SERVICES • GENERAL SETTINGS • ACTIVATE SAP GTS ACCELERATOR.

Activating the SAP GTS Accelerator allows you to access the relevant data in the SAP HANA database as quickly as possible. After starting the relevant report program in the SAP area menu, the data is immediately available for analysis and further processing. The following SAP GTS Accelerators are available:

- ▶ GTS Accelerator for audit trail
- ▶ GTS Accelerator for blocked business partners
- ▶ GTS Accelerator for blocked documents

When you first enter the configuration screen, click on NEW ENTRIES to bring up the image in Figure 3.1. You will have to select one of the three available options and then check off the box next to ACTIVE. You will also have to enter the name of the database as a native SQL CONNECT statement.

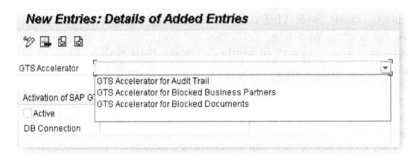

Figure 3.1: Activate SAP GTS Accelerator

3.1.2 Activate alert monitoring

In this customizing step, activate alert monitors. Alert monitors are a part of SAP Computing Center Management System (CCMS).

You can choose from the following alert monitors:

- ▶ Communication with feeder system
- ▶ Communication with customs authorities systems
- ▶ General processing in SAP GTS

Depending on which message type is selected, you can define at which message level the alert is triggered.

You can define which objects and sub-objects the alert takes into consideration.

To activate these monitors, follow the menu path SPRO • SAP REFERENCE IMG • GLOBAL TRADE SERVICES • GENERAL SETTINGS • ACTIVATE ALERT MONITORING.

You can see this screen in Figure 3.2. When you enter the screen, you must select NEW ENTRIES to activate monitoring. Choose an OBJECT and a SUB OBJECT within that object. Next, choose a MESSAGE TYPE and an ALERT MONITOR. Once they are selected, you have selected and activated a unique set of circumstances to monitor. The example in Figure 3.2 shows the following:

- ▶ OBJECT: SAP GTS: Preference
- ▶ SUB OBJECT: Maintain vendor declarations
- ▶ MESSAGE TYPE: Error message
- ▶ ALERT MONITOR: General processing in SAP GTS

This means that an alert will be caused any time an error message occurs in the MAINTAIN VENDOR DECLARATIONS area of GTS.

You will see the available OBJECTS in Figure 3.2. Each object has its own SUB OBJECTS, which are too numerous to list. Figure 3.3 shows the available MESSAGE TYPES.

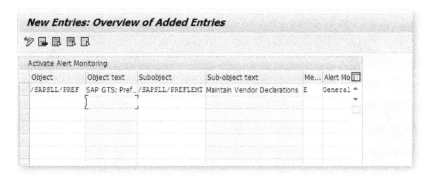

Figure 3.2: Activate alert monitoring

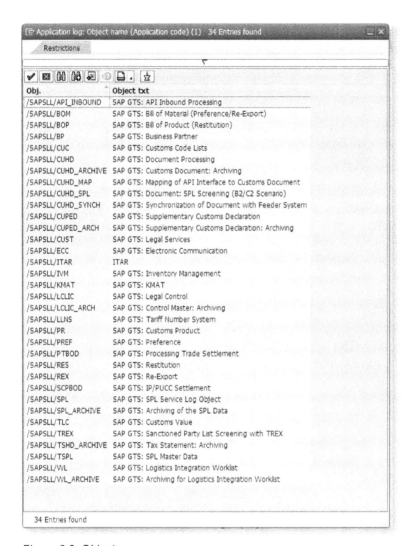

Figure 3.3: Objects

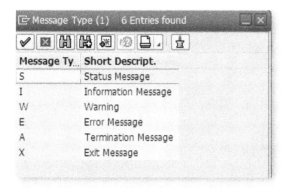

Figure 3.4: Message types

3.1.3 Number ranges

GTS previously had a number ranges section in the configuration where you could set up ranges for varied numbers as partners or documents. There is a new option in SAP GTS 11.0 to support the new foreign trade zone (FTZ) functionality. This can be accessed through the menu path SPRO • SAP REFERENCE IMG • GLOBAL TRADE SERVICES • GENERAL SETTINGS • NUMBER RANGES • DEFINE NUMBER RANGES FOR CONSOLIDATED COMPLETIONS FOR CUSTOMS WAREHOUSE (see Figure 3.5).

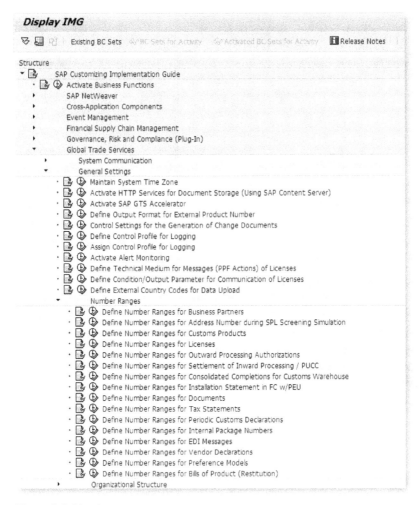

Figure 3.5: Number ranges

When you enter this number ranges configuration screen, you can create or review existing number ranges; see Figure 3.6.

Figure 3.6: Maintain number range

You can create a new range on this screen. The key settings/options are:

NO: This is the interval. Selecting "1" means that the number climbs in increments of one (such as 1, 2, 3, 4).

YEAR: The year you want this range to be effective.

FROM NO: The beginning of the range.

TO NUMBER: The end of the range.

NR STATUS: The highest currently used number in the range.

EXT: Whether the range is internal (unchecked) or external (checked).

3.2   In-memory optimization

One of SAP HANA's key benefits is its in-memory functionality and the increased performance that it brings. *In-memory* means that the computer processor performs the database functionalities within its main memory, as opposed to accessing a disk storage system. This results in much quicker response times, since CPU speed has increased in the last twenty years nearly 50 times more than disk data transfer systems have. As a result, CPU memory speed is now much faster than disk speed.[3] This means users can expect:

▶ Improved performance in key go-to market (GTM) processes such as e-commerce.

▶ Enhanced reporting and analytics capabilities for global trade activities.

3.2.1   Solution enhancement

You can expect the following enhancements with SAP HANA and GTS working together:

▶ Key processes in customs, compliance, and preference enhanced to leverage the SAP HANA database for improved response time and performance.

▶ New SPL search algorithm to leverage HANA performance (see Section 3.3 for more on this).

▶ Robust search capabilities to improve data-intensive processes such as classification.

▶ Broader availability of operational trade data for use in analytics based on SAP HANA.

3.2.2   Key benefits

These enhancements will deliver the following key benefits:

---

[3] "What is SAP HANA?", accessed February 26, 2015, http://scn.sap.com/docs/ DOC-60338

▶ Enhanced operational performance in global trade processes.

▶ Dramatic improvement in global trade reporting response time.

▶ Analytics spans across applications of SAP Business Suite application (integrated analytics).

▶ Full ability to leverage in-memory database investment across the enterprise, including global trade management activities.

3.3   SPL with HANA Search

As discussed already, SAP HANA is a significant new feature for SAP GTS with 11.0. No function is more affected than SPL. With 11.0 and HANA, there are three noticeable improvements to SPL.

Benefits of SAP HANA Search

▶ Simplified SPL set-up

▶ Simplified SPL use

▶ Improved performance

3.3.1   Simplified SPL setup

SAP GTS 11.0 now provides three options for setting up sanctioned party list screening.

▶ Classic SPL algorithm within SAP GTS ("SAP GTS Search")

▶ TREX search along with classic SPL algorithm ("SAP TREX Search")

▶ SAP HANA Search

You can see the options in Figure 3.7. The first two choices are identical to what previous TREX compatible versions had. The third choice is new to 11.0 and requires HANA. This options is available following menu path SPRO • SAP REFERENCE IMG • GLOBAL TRADE SERVICES • COMPLIANCE MANAGEMENT • SANCTIONED PARTY LIST SCREENING • DEFINE COMPARISON PROCEDURE.

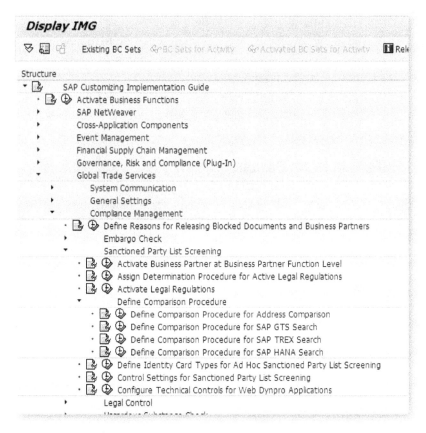

Figure 3.7: New SPL options

Setting up SPL with HANA requires far fewer actions and choices. As you can see in Figure 3.8 there are fewer decisions to make. You simply choose a screening pattern and the percentage thresholds you want to set. The screening pattern replaces the old selection of fields for screening. Rather than set up and activate fields to screen, you simply choose from a predefined list of sets, as shown in Figure 3.9.

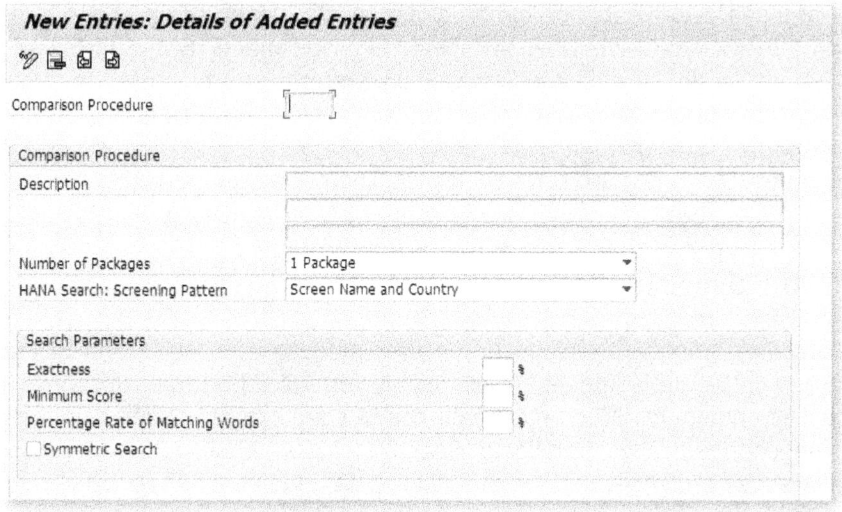

New Entries: Details of Added Entries

Comparison Procedure

Comparison Procedure

Description

Number of Packages   1 Package
HANA Search: Screening Pattern   Screen Name and Country

Search Parameters

Exactness   %
Minimum Score   %
Percentage Rate of Matching Words   %
☐ Symmetric Search

Figure 3.8: SPL HANA settings

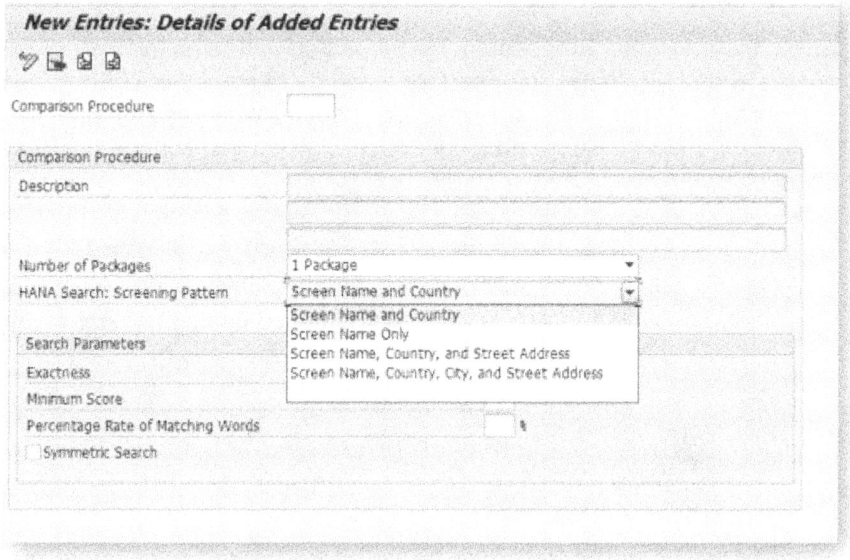

New Entries: Details of Added Entries

Comparison Procedure

Comparison Procedure

Description

Number of Packages   1 Package
HANA Search: Screening Pattern   Screen Name and Country

Screen Name and Country
Screen Name Only
Screen Name, Country, and Street Address
Screen Name, Country, City, and Street Address

Search Parameters

Exactness
Minimum Score
Percentage Rate of Matching Words   %
☐ Symmetric Search

Figure 3.9: Screening patterns

For those who want to define a unique set of fields to screen not offered by these choices, the other two methods (traditional GTS and TREX) are still available. All of the customization and choices found in the older versions are still available. However, with HANA, you can configure and begin SPL screening in much less time. Furthermore, as you will see in the next two sections, HANA brings with it other efficiencies.

3.3.2 Simplified SPL use

The most important change to the user process with HANA and SPL is when SPL data is updated. Most installations of GTS have subscription-based content for SPL. This means the lists are constantly being updated and changed. With traditional SAP GTS, after each content change, there was a complicated set of master data updates that had to be managed to rebuild indexes.

Similarly, any time the business partner data was updated, you needed to recreate the comparison terms.

Unlike the traditional SPL search, HANA search optimizes this part of the operation and eliminates the need for those extra steps. As you can see in Figure 3.10, four steps are no longer needed when you update SPL content, and two steps are no longer needed when you change business partners.

Figure 3.10: Unnecessary steps with HANA

3.3.3 Improved performance

As discussed in Section 3.2, SAP HANA is a much faster database tool than traditional disk-based systems. As a result, SPL screenings will occur much more quickly. This improved performance will result in business efficiencies, as well as greater compliance.

3.4 Enhanced user experience

Next to HANA, perhaps the most exciting recent development in the SAP realm has been *Fiori*. According to SAP, "SAP Fiori is the new user experience (UX) for SAP software that applies modern design principles."[4] To put this in plain English, SAP Fiori brings the pleasant visuals and easily navigated interfaces that users have come to expect from other technology such as their smart phones. In other words, it is easy and quick to use!

3.4.1 Solution enhancement

SAP Fiori apps are user-friendly and quicker to navigate. You can expect the following enhancements with SAP GTS 11.0:

- ▶ Easy-to-understand format for metrics and dashboards.
- ▶ Customization of information used for key performance indicators (KPIs) to match business needs and user roles.
- ▶ The ability to drill down and take action where needed.

3.4.2 Key benefits

These user interface enhancements will bring the following benefits:

- ▶ Customizable KPI tiles keep the most important information up-front.
- ▶ Ability to leverage launchpad in SAP Fiori apps to organize a user's areas to monitor.
- ▶ Integrates with transactional SAP Fiori apps to make insight actionable.

---

[4] "SAP Fiori UX", accessed July 7, 2015,
http://help.sap.com/fiori_bs2013/helpdata/en/84/154353a7ace547e10000000a441470/frameset.htm

Figure 3.11 shows a few examples of how SAP GTS and SAP Fiori will look.

Figure 3.11: SAP Fiori and SAP GTS

3.5 FTZ

SAP GTS 11.0 will support the operation of a foreign trade zone (FTZ) in the USA, something that many SAP GTS users have been requesting. It will also allow for integration of FTZ functions with other back end systems for current FTZ operators and offers some enhancements.

Figure 3.12 shows the new menu options for FTZ in CUSTOMS MANAGEMENT.

3.5.1 Solution enhancement

Version 11.0 brings several solution enhancements related to FTZ operations. They include:

► Automated tracking of the inventories held in FTZ.
► Accurate consumption of inventories related to manufacturing manufacture within an FTZ.

- ▶ Interfaces with US customs to report goods movement in and out of an FTZ (electronic communication).
- ▶ Supports processes related to import and export with zones.

3.5.2 Key benefits

FTZ brings valuable customs processing and cash flow benefits to users. Some of the greatest benefits you can get from an FTZ (with or without SAP GTS) are:

General FTZ benefits

- ▶ Duty deferral – No duties paid until goods enter commerce of the US.
- ▶ Duty elimination – No duties paid if goods never enter US commerce.
- ▶ Inverted tax relief – Pay duties on the manufactured good tariff rate.
- ▶ Customs fee reductions – Reduce merchandise processing fees.
- ▶ Ad valorem tax relief – No inventory tax on goods in an FTZ.

Beyond the benefits that an FTZ brings on its own, using SAP GTS with an FTZ maximizes your efficiency. The unique benefits SAP GTS can bring to an FTZ user include:

- ▶ Reduced duty costs associated with the import of goods and component.
- ▶ Reduced expenses associated with operating in an FTZ due to manual tracking and reporting of inventory, manufacture, and movements.
- ▶ Improved data accuracy through full integration with back-end systems of record.
- ▶ Faster processing through certified interfaces with US customs.
- ▶ Enable high-volume processing through FTZs by leveraging in-memory technology.

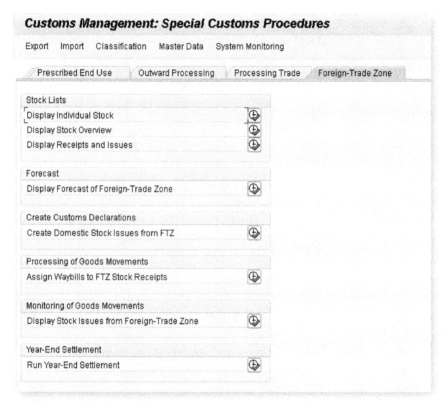

Figure 3.12: FTZ in the SAP GTS Cockpit

3.6 Customs management improvements

3.6.1 Customs management: Import – new waybill tab

SAP GTS 11.0 has new waybill functionality. This is a new tab in the CUSTOMS MANAGEMENT • IMPORT area (see Figure 3.13). In SAP GTS, you will now be able to view waybills, as well as create and edit them.

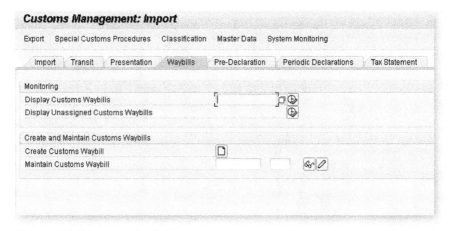

Figure 3.13: New waybill tab in customs management

3.6.2 Special customs procedures: foreign trade zone

As discussed in Section 3.5, SAP GTS 11.0 includes new FTZ functionality. This also includes some changes to the SAP GTS CUSTOMS MANAGEMENT area.

As you can see in Figure 3.12, it appears as a new tab in the CUSTOMS MANAGEMENT • SPECIAL CUSTOMS PROCEDURES area.

3.6.3 Product maintenance

There are several changes to the way product classification looks and works.

Icons removed from tabs

This is a simple visual change, but there are no longer icons in the tab headers. The change allows more tabs to be visible at once because they take up less space (see Figure 3.14).

Product short texts moved to new commercial description tab

There is a new tab called COMMERCIAL DESCRIPTION. Here, rather than having a single product description per language, you can have separate descriptions by country regardless of language (see Figure 3.14).

Figure 3.14: New edit products screen

Special customs procedures tab redesigned

As you can see in Figure 3.15, there are new features in customs management to support FTZ functionality.

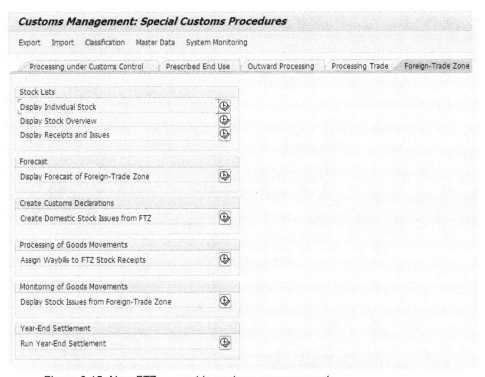

Figure 3.15: New FTZ support in customs management

3.7 Improvements to compliance management

3.7.1 Sanctioned party list – exclude deleted business partners

In SAP GTS 11.0, business partners (BP) that are deleted or marked for deletion in the feeder system will no longer be considered valid for screening. Existing SAP GTS functionality allowed you to exclude expired SPL entries, but not BP. The system would check a BP, even if it had been marked for deletion. In SAP GTS 11.0, BP deleted or marked for deletion are given a truncated valid-to date, making the partner obsolete provided the exclude expired address is selected (see Figure 3.16).

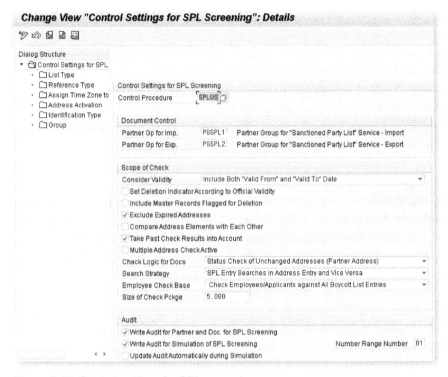

Figure 3.16: Control settings for SPL screening

3.7.2 Legal control

License determination – all partner types

Previous versions of SAP GTS only use the first partner function in a partner group and customs document used for license determination. SAP GTS 11.0 carries out license determination for all partner functions available in a partner group and customs document.

If the same license is determined for several partner functions, the license assignment including depreciation only occurs once.

Check multiple license types in all determination strategies

In previous versions, MULTIPLE LICENSE CHECK was merely a toggle on or off. Now if the multiple license type check is enabled, GTS checks and assigns licenses in terms of determination strategy. This is done in the CONTROL SETTINGS FOR LEGAL CONTROL section of configuration and can be seen in Figure 3.17.

CHECK IN ONE DETERMINATION STRATEGY: The system releases the document if the licenses under all the license types are successfully determined and assigned in one of determination strategies. This is the old system behavior.

CHECK IN ALL DETERMINATION STRATEGIES: The system releases the document if the licenses under all the license types are successfully determined and assigned in all the determination strategies. The function is enabled as of release SLL-LEG 900 SP22 and SLL-LEG 901 SP14.

Figure 3.17: Multiple license check

Values and quantities at control class or import code number

Under some laws, customs approves the total amount of values and quantities at the control class or import code number level. SAP GTS 11.0 enables the maintenance of license values and quantities at the control class or import code number level and depreciates values and quantities on the same two levels. Figure 3.18 provides an overview of this new setup.

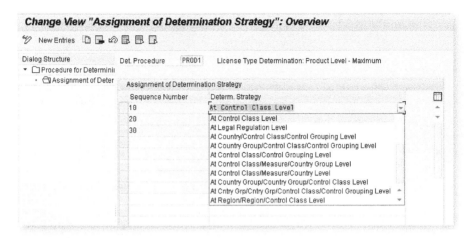

Figure 3.18: Determination strategy assignment

3.8   Preference improvements

3.8.1   Utilize simulation of preference determination for analysis

Previous SAP GTS versions only allowed simulation in dialog mode, so the results were not persisted or maintained.

SAP GTS 11.0 enables:

- ▶ Persistence of simulation in a log.
- ▶ Execution of simulation in dialog or background.
- ▶ Analysis of simulated origin information in simulation logs in parallel with productive origin information stored in SAP GTS product master.

You will notice in Figure 3.19 that there is now a SAVE LOG option next to SIMULATION that was not in previous versions.

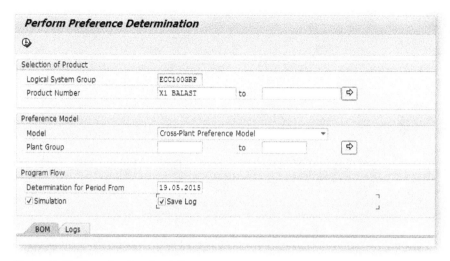

Figure 3.19: Save log for simulation

4 Appendix 1: SPL list types and references

The table below lists common lists that businesses screen against. The list codes are from MK Data Services and are used with permission. Next to each list code is a description explaining what the list is, in addition to a website where the user can go for further information.

This is meant to be a tool that you can incorporate into your company's SPL compliance program. When you have a potential match against one of these lists, you can go to the website to better understand:

- ▶ If you have a true match, and
- ▶ What the significance of the list is.

This table is not a complete list of SPL offerings. It is intended to show the most common and most important lists, and to assist you as you customize your own internal training program. Since lists change frequently (some are delisted and new ones are created) this is not meant to be a static tool—you must review it and keep it updated constantly. It is our hope that this will give you the start of a good tool and point you in the right direction.

List	Description	Direct website link to source list and information
561L	List of Foreign Financial Institutions (OFAC)	*http://sdnsearch.ofac.treas.gov/*
ACL	Australian Consolidated List	*http://dfat.gov.au/international-relations/security/sanctions/Pages/sanctions.aspx*
ATFMW	ATF & Explosives Most Wanted	*https://www.atf.gov/content/ATF-most-wanted*
BALK	SDN, Western Balkans (OFAC)	*http://sdnsearch.ofac.treas.gov/*
BOE	Bank of England—Financial Sanctions (HM Treasury)	*http://www.hm-treasury.gov.uk/fin_sanctions_index.htm*

List	Description	Direct website link to source list and information
CBW	Chemical Biological Weapons Concerns (DOS)	http://www.state.gov/t/isn/c15231.htm
COTED	Specially Designated National Cote d'Ivoire(OFAC)	http://sdnsearch.ofac.treas.gov/
CTL	Canadian Restricted Entities	http://www.international.gc.ca/sanctions/countries-pays/index.aspx?lang=eng
DEAMW	Drug Enforcement Administration	http://www.dea.gov/fugitives.shtml
DOS	Department of State Debarred Parties	http://www.pmddtc.state.gov/compliance/debar_intro.html
DTO	Designated Terrorist Organization (DOS/OFAC)	http://sdnsearch.ofac.treas.gov/
ERL	End-User Requiring License-Entity List (BXA)	http://export.gov/ecr/eg_main_023148.asp
EUS	European Sanctions List	http://eeas.europa.eu/cfsp/sanctions/consol-list_en.htm
FBI	FBI Most Wanted List	http://www.fbi.gov/wanted
FINC	Money Laundering Concerns (FINCEN)	http://www.fincen.gov/statutes_regs/patriot/section311.html
GSA	GSA Debarred bidders list— reciprocal	www.sam.gov
INPA	Iran Non-proliferation Act	http://www.state.gov/t/isn/c15231.htm
INPOL	Interpol—Wanted Persons	http://www.interpol.int/notice/search/wanted
ISA	Iran Sanctions Act	http://www.state.gov/t/isn/c15231.htm

List	Description	Direct website link to source list and information
ISNA	Iran and Syria Non-proliferation Act	*http://www.state.gov/t/isn/c15231.htm*
MT	Missile Technology Concerns (DOS)	*http://www.state.gov/t/isn/c15231.htm*
MVC	Merchant Vessel, Cuba (OFAC)	*http://sdnsearch.ofac.treas.gov/*
NPWMD	Non-proliferation Weapons Of Mass Destruction	*http://sdnsearch.ofac.treas.gov/*
NSPLC	Non-SDN Palestinian Legislative Council (OFAC)	*http://sdnsearch.ofac.treas.gov/*
RFC	Red Flag Concerns (BIS Unverified List)	*http://export.gov/ecr/eg_main_023148.asp*
SDGT	Specially Designated Global Terrorist SDGT (OFAC)	*http://sdnsearch.ofac.treas.gov/*
SDME	Specially Designated Terrorists—SDME	*http://sdnsearch.ofac.treas.gov/*
SDNB	Specially Designated Nationals, Belarus (OFAC)	*http://sdnsearch.ofac.treas.gov/*
SDNC	Specially Designated Nationals, Cuba (OFAC)	*http://sdnsearch.ofac.treas.gov/*
SDNK	Specially Designated Nationals, N. Korea (OFAC)	*http://sdnsearch.ofac.treas.gov/*

List	Description	Direct website link to source list and information
SDNL	Specially Designated Nationals, Libya (OFAC)	*http://sdnsearch.ofac.treas.gov/*
SDNLB	Specially Designated Nationals, Lebanon (OFAC)	*http://sdnsearch.ofac.treas.gov/*
SDNLR	Specially Designated Nationals, Liberia (OFAC)	*http://sdnsearch.ofac.treas.gov/*
SDNR	Specially Designated Nationals, Iran (OFAC)	*http://sdnsearch.ofac.treas.gov/*
SDNS	Specially Designated Nationals, Sudan (OFAC)	*http://sdnsearch.ofac.treas.gov/*
SDNSO	Specially Designated Nationals, Somalia (OFAC)	*http://sdnsearch.ofac.treas.gov/*
SDNSY	Specially Designated Nationals, Syria (OFAC)	*http://sdnsearch.ofac.treas.gov/*
SDNT	Specially Designated Narcotics Trafficker	*http://sdnsearch.ofac.treas.gov/*
SECO	Swiss Restricted List	*http://www.seco.admin.ch/index.html ?lang=en*
TCO	Transnational Criminal Organisations (OFAC)	*http://sdnsearch.ofac.treas.gov/*

List	Description	Direct website link to source list and information
TDO	Denied Persons List (BIS) Commerce Dept. Denial List	*http://export.gov/ecr/eg_main_023148.asp*
UKPC	UK Proliferation Concerns (Concern List Only)	*https://www.gov.uk/international-non-proliferation-and-arms-control-regimes*
UNS	United Nations Security Council Sanctions	*http://www.un.org/sc/committees/list_compend.shtml*
WB	World Bank — List of Disbarred/Ineligible Firms	*http://www.worldbank.org/debarr*

5 Appendix 2: Website resources

The following lists of websites are publicly available sites, where you can research various relevant topics. They are sorted by key categories. This list will be useful as you perform your master data set up and classifications. It will also lead you to sites that further explain various concepts discussed in this book.

5.1 Sanctioned party list resources

Hyperlink	Description	Country
http://export.gov/ecr/eg_main_023148.asp	Three Agency Consolidated Screening List (Downloadable)	USA
https://sdnsearch.ofac.treas.gov/	Department of Treasury Search Tool	USA
https://www.sam.gov	GSA Debarred Entity Search Tool	USA
http://www.un.org/sc/committees/list_compend.shtml	Security Council Sanctions (Downloadable)	UN
http://eeas.europa.eu/cfsp/sanctions/consol-list/index_en.htm	EU Sanctioned Parties (Downloadable)	EU

5.2   Preferential trade resources

Hyperlink	Description	Country
https://www.nafta-sec-alena.org/	NAFTA Secretariat	NAFTA
https://www.acquisition.gov/	Federal Acquisition Regulation (FAR)	USA
http://www.dot.gov/highlights/buyamerica	Buy America Requirements	USA
https://www.ftc.gov/tips-advice/business-center/guidance/complying-made-usa-standard	FTC "Made In USA" Requirements	USA
http://www.cbp.gov/sites/default/files/documents/Side-by-Side%2C%20Final%207%2716%2714.pdf	US List of Free Trade Agreements (Side by Side)	USA
http://ptadb.wto.org/	WTO Preferential Trade Page	UN
http://ec.europa.eu/enterprise/policies/international/facilitating-trade/free-trade/index_en.htm	EU Free Trade Agreement Page	EU
http://www.international.gc.ca/trade-agreements-accords-commerciaux/agr-acc/fta-ale.aspx?lang=eng	Canada List of Free Trade Agreements	CA

5.3   Export/import control resources

Hyperlink	Description	Country
http://www.bis.doc.gov/index.php/licensing/commerce-control-list-classification/export-control-classification-number-eccn	BIS ECCN Classification Page	USA
https://www.bis.doc.gov/index.php/regulations/export-administration-regulations-ear	Export Administration Regulations	USA

Hyperlink	Description	Country
https://www.pmddtc.state.gov/regulations_laws/itar.html	Department Of State ITAR Page	USA
http://www.international.gc.ca/controls-controles/about-a_propos/expor/guide.aspx?lang=eng	Canadian Export Control System	CA
http://ec.europa.eu/trade/import-and-export-rules/export-from-eu/dual-use-controls/	EU Export Controls Page	EU
http://www.wassenaar.org/	Wassenaar Arrangement Page	Multi.
http://www.australiagroup.net/en/index.html	Australia Group Page	Multi.

5.4 Customs compliance resources

Hyperlink	Description	Country
http://www.cbp.gov/	US Customs And Border Protection	US
http://www.cbsa-asfc.gc.ca/	Canada Border Services Agency	CA
http://ec.europa.eu/taxation_customs/index_en.htm	EU Customs Union	EU
http://www.wcoomd.org/	World Customs Organization	UN

You have finished the book.

A   About the Authors

© Lauren DeVries 2015

Kevin Riddell, CCLP is the International Logistics Manager, North America for The Tremco Group, where he has worked for more than 20 years. The Tremco Group manufactures and exports chemical-based construction products worldwide. Kevin is responsible for International Trade Compliance, including Customs Compliance and related import and export regulations. Kevin is the business lead and administrator for SAP GTS, and led the software selection/implementation process in 2011.

Kevin lives in Toronto, Canada and splits his work time between Toronto and Cleveland, Ohio. He is a regular presenter on SAP GTS as well as Trade Compliance, and he speaks at both SAP and non-SAP events.

Rajen Iyer, CPIM, PMP is the Co-Founder and CTO at Krypt, Inc., one of the fastest growing Global Trade and Supply Chain solution providers with innovative products and services and a global presence. Mr. Iyer is a thought leader and has authored several best-selling books and in-depth articles. He holds a number of IP and trademarks on trade, logistics, and supply chain products. With an educational background in engineering and management, his experience spans strategic, business and system consulting, product development, and implementation. He is frequently invited to speak at industry conferences and is a licensed customs broker.

B Index

C Disclaimer

This publication contains references to the products of SAP SE.

SAP, R/3, SAP NetWeaver, Duet, PartnerEdge, ByDesign, SAP BusinessObjects Explorer, StreamWork, and other SAP products and services mentioned herein as well as their respective logos are trademarks or registered trademarks of SAP SE in Germany and other countries.

Business Objects and the Business Objects logo, BusinessObjects, Crystal Reports, Crystal Decisions, Web Intelligence, Xcelsius, and other Business Objects products and services mentioned herein as well as their respective logos are trademarks or registered trademarks of Business Objects Software Ltd. Business Objects is an SAP company.

Sybase and Adaptive Server, iAnywhere, Sybase 365, SQL Anywhere, and other Sybase products and services mentioned herein as well as their respective logos are trademarks or registered trademarks of Sybase, Inc. Sybase is an SAP company.

SAP SE is neither the author nor the publisher of this publication and is not responsible for its content. SAP Group shall not be liable for errors or omissions with respect to the materials. The only warranties for SAP Group products and services are those that are set forth in the express warranty statements accompanying such products and services, if any. Nothing herein should be construed as constituting an additional warranty.

More Espresso Tutorials Books

Claudia Jost:

First Steps in the SAP® Purchasing Processes (MM)

▶ Compact manual for the SAP procurement processes

▶ Comprehensive example with numerous illustrations

▶ Master data, purchase requirements and goods receipt in context

http://5016.espresso-tutorials.com

Matthew Johnson:

SAP® Material Master—A Practical Guide

▶ Understand SAP Master concepts

▶ Maximize your value stream through SAP Materials Management (MM)

▶ Walk through practical implementation examples

http://5028.espresso-tutorials.com

Björn Weber:

First Steps in the SAP® Production Processes (PP)

▶ Compact manual for discrete production in SAP

▶ Comprehensive example with numerous illustrations

▶ Master data, resource planning and production orders in context

http://5027.espresso-tutorials.com

Tobias Götz, Anette Götz:

Practical Guide to Transportation Management with SAP®

▶ Supported business processes

▶ Best practices

▶ Integration aspects and architecture

▶ Comparison and differentiation to similar SAP components

http://5082.espresso-tutorials.com

Avijt Dutta & Shreekant Shiralkar:

Demand Planning with SAP® APO—Concepts and Design

▶ Step-by-Step Explanations and Easy to Follow Instructions

▶ Combination of Theory, Business Relevance and 'How to' Approach

▶ APO DP Concepts and Design Explained using a Business Scenario

▶ Centralized Process Flow Diagram to Illustrate Integration

http://5105.espresso-tutorials.com

Avijt Dutta & Shreekant Shiralkar:

Demand Planning with SAP® APO—Execution

▶ Step-by-Step Explanations and Easy to Follow Instructions

▶ Combination of Theory, Business Relevance and 'How to' Approach

▶ APO DP Execution Explained using a Business Scenario

▶ Centralized Process Flow Diagram to Illustrate Integration

http://5106.espresso-tutorials.com

www.ingramcontent.com/pod-product-compliance
Lightning Source LLC
Chambersburg PA
CBHW071110050326
40690CB00008B/1181